WHAT IS A BRIDGE?

WHAT IS A BRIDGE?

THE MAKING OF CALATRAVA'S BRIDGE IN SEVILLE

SPIRO N. POLLALIS   drawings by Alberto Diaz-Hermidas   The MIT Press · Cambridge, Massachusetts · London, England

CONTENTS

This book was set in Scala FF and DIN by Graphic Composi-
tion, Inc., Athens, Georgia, and was printed and bound in
the United States of America.

Library of Congress Cataloging-in-Publication Data

Pollalis, Spiro N., 1954–
    What is a bridge? : the making of Calatrava's bridge in
Seville / Spiro N. Pollalis ; drawings by Alberto Diaz-
Hermidas.
        p.   cm.
    Includes bibliographical references.
    ISBN 0-262-16174-5 (hc : alk. paper)
    1. Puente del Alamillo (Seville, Spain).   2. Bridges—
Spain—Seville—Design and construction.   I. Title.
TG88.P84P65   1999
624'.5.094686—dc21   98-53516
                                                    CIP

PREFACE

In 1992, Spain was celebrating full membership in the European Union, the quincentennial of the discovery of the Americas, the Olympic Games in Barcelona, and the Universal Exposition in Seville. In that exciting environment, a time of intensive architectural activities resulting from a reconstruction of the infrastructure of the country, the harp-shaped Alamillo Bridge rose to a height of 142 meters. Its design became the symbol of the city of Seville and attracted international attention.

The Alamillo Bridge is among Santiago Calatrava's most eminent bridges, with strong archi-

Alamillo Bridge in Seville. That bridge was selected because it pushes engineering and construction to unprecedented frontiers, while its design merit has been widely acknowledged. An architectural model of the bridge is in the collection of the Museum of Modern Art in New York.

The design, engineering, and construction of the Alamillo Bridge are presented here step by step. After the first design schemes are introduced, the conceptual design is explained in depth, with an emphasis on its architectural and technical innovations. Then the constructed design is presented, accompanied by the engineering analysis, the construction process employed, and the related technical issues. The Alamillo Bridge is placed in the context of the rest of Calatrava's work, and parallels are drawn to the work of other artists, architects, and engineers.

tectural intentions and ambitious engineering, made possible through the intimate collaboration of a supporting patron, brilliant engineers, and daring contractors. With a single oblique pylon without backstays, the 200-meter-long cable-stayed bridge exemplifies organic form, equilibrium, and precision in construction like no other contemporary bridge.

Calatrava's powerful shapes have attracted the attention of the architectural press, and numerous articles and books have been written on his work. Although most of those describe his work as spanning architecture and engineering, they do not provide an in-depth treatment of the work in terms of engineering and construction.

This book follows a different approach. Acknowledging the need to pay attention to both architecture and engineering and the inherent complexity of doing so, the book focuses on a single project: the design and construction of the

ACKNOWLEDGMENTS

In 1987, I met Santiago Calatrava in Zurich. My colleague Professor Herbert Kramel from the ETH-Zürich had introduced me to him following our discussions of how, as technology matures, uncertainty in bridge design shifts toward subjective design intentions. That first meeting was electrifying, and I was convinced that Santiago would transform bridge design forever. After that we met several times more and in the summer of 1988 we started working together in Zurich. One of the projects was the Alamillo Bridge in Seville, which was completed when I was part of the new office in Paris, during my leave of absence from Harvard, in 1991–1992. From the very beginning, I had an interest in writing a monograph on the bridge as a single piece of work that epitomizes Calatrava's approach to design.

Starting in the summer of 1990, my doctoral student Alberto Diaz-Hermidas visited the site in Seville several times to sketch the construction of the bridge. He also researched the design and construction process of the bridge and made many line drawings which, in addition to his sketches, illustrate this book.

A number of people and organizations were instrumental in the development of this book. Santiago and Tina Calatrava were very helpful throughout the project. Intecsa, Dragados y Construcciones SA, Fomento de Construcciones y Contratas SA, Florida Wire and Cable Co., and Dywidag Systems International provided information on the project. Professor Carlos Alonso-Cobo provided the detailed engineering analysis, and the Junta of Andalucía gave me access to many documents related to the bridge as well as the complete set of the construction drawings. Alberto Diaz-Fraga facilitated the gathering of original information from various sources in Spain. The office of Santiago Calatrava was supportive and provided the original drawings for the bridge. During the unfolding of this project, I was impressed once more by the open-mindedness of the Junta de Andalucía in commissioning the bridge, and the willingness of the Spanish architects, engineers, and contractors to explore new concepts and challenge old practices.

I would like to thank my colleagues, Daniel Schodek of Harvard University, Christian Menn and Hans Hauri of the ETH-Zürich, Alex Tzonis and Liane Lefaivre of TU-Delft, and Michael Kavvadas of the Technical University of Athens, as well as Juan Manuel Moron of Dragados y Construcciones SA, for the insightful exchange of ideas on bridge design, technology, and architecture, as well as for reviewing the manuscript.

In addition, I would like to thank my student Murray Monroe for duplicating the finite element analysis. Finally, I thank Paolo Rosselli and Heinrich Helfenstein, whose photographs add significantly to the visual material of the book.

Spiro N. Pollalis
Poros, Greece, 1998
pollalis@gsd.harvard.edu
www.gsd.harvard.edu/~pollalis

WHAT IS A BRIDGE?

1 THE COMMISSION FOR THE ALAMILLO BRIDGE

In 1987 the Junta de Andalucía, the local government of one of the seventeen autonomous regions of Spain, commissioned Santiago Calatrava to design the Alamillo Bridge in Seville (fig. 1.1). The selection of Calatrava as the bridge's designer emphasized the Junta's commitment to signature architecture of public works. The bridge was part of a new roadway linking Seville with the towns and villages located west of the city (fig. 1.2). The new roadway would also serve as one of the three main access routes from

Seville to the 1992 Universal Exposition (Expo '92), providing access to the North Gate of the exposition area.

No bridges had been built over the Guadalquivir river in the city of Seville since 1964. On the occasion of Expo '92, six new bridges were commissioned to improve the infrastructure of the city (table 1.1). Three of those bridges provided a direct link from Seville to the Expo '92 grounds: the Barqueta Bridge, at the Barqueta Gate of Expo '92,

commissioned to Juan José Arenas and Marcos J. Pantaleón (fig. 1.3); the Cartuja Bridge at the Cartuja Gate, the main entrance to Expo '92, commissioned to Fritz Leonhardt and Luis Viñuela (fig. 1.4); and El Cachorro Bridge, providing access to the South Gate, commissioned to José Luis Manzanares (fig. 1.5). Further south, Las Delicias Bridge was commissioned to Leonardo Fernández and Javier Monterola (fig. 1.6), while the Fifth Centenary Bridge was commissioned to José A. Fer-

nández Ordóñez and Julio Martínez Calzón (fig. 1.7).

Among those six new bridges, the Alamillo Bridge had the least prestigious location, close to a depressed neighborhood, and was least visible from the city. However, it has captured most of the

| **Fig. 1.1** | The Alamillo Bridge in Seville. Photo by Paolo Rosselli. |

attention, not only among the bridges built for Expo '92 but among all the buildings erected for the exposition, including the pavilions. This is particularly interesting since most of the buildings and the pavilions were designed by prominent and celebrated architects.[1]

1 For a detailed description of the 111 pavilions and buildings, see *Expo'92 Seville: Architecture and Design* (Milan: Electa, 1993). Calatrava designed the Kuwait pavilion, a commission awarded in 1991.

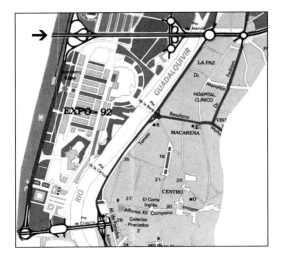

Fig. 1.2 | The alignment of the roadway of the Alamillo Bridge.

Table 1.1 The six bridges built in Seville as part of the improvement of the infrastructure for Expo '92.

Bridge	Designers	Type	Span (m)	Clear span (m)	Width (m)
Alamillo	S. Calatrava	cable-stayed, single pylon	220	185	32
Barqueta	J. J. Arenas and M. J. Pantaleón	high arch	168	168	21
Cartuja	F. Leonhardt and L. Viñuela	beam box	238	170	25
El Cachorro	J. L. Manzanares	shallow arch	220	220	31
Las Delicias	L. Fernández and J. Monterola	bascule	160	56	27
Fifth Centenary	J. Fernández-Ordóñez and J. Martínez Calzón	cable-stayed, two pylons	2,018	265	22

Fig. 1.3 | The Barqueta Bridge.

Fig. 1.4 | The Cartuja Bridge.

Fig. 1.5 | El Cachorro Bridge.

Fig. 1.6 | Las Delicias Bridge.

Fig. 1.7 | The Fifth Centenary Bridge.

1.1
CALATRAVA'S SELECTION AS THE DESIGNER OF THE ALAMILLO BRIDGE

The commission for the Alamillo Bridge was given to Calatrava by way of a provision in Spanish law stating that direct commissions can be given to prominent architects of international recognition, without the requirement of an official competition or competitive bidding. Calatrava, a Spanish architect and engineer who was practicing in Zurich, had earned that international recognition. His practice has had a phenomenal success since it opened in 1982. His designs have greatly influenced the design approach to bridges, canopies, and large enclosed spaces. However, his most significant contribution has been in transforming the traditional engineering field of bridge design by following a clearly architectural trajectory. Calatrava's early influence on bridge design also fueled many discussions on the relation between architecture and engineering that extended beyond bridges.

In 1987, he had just completed his famous Felipe II Bridge in the Bach de Roda neighborhood of Barcelona (see Nolli, 1987). That bridge provided a precedent in innovative bridge design from an architectural perspective, and demonstrated the capabilities of Calatrava's architectural and engineering office. The creation of three-dimensional space by the bridge's structural elements was unprecedented (fig. 1.8). Four arches, two on each side of the bridge, form its structural system. The vertical arches that border the roadway define the space for vehicular traffic, a space unobstructed and thus suitable for quite tall vehicles. The lateral stability of the vertical arches is ensured by the inclined arches that create large balcony-like spaces on either side of the bridge. Those spaces, articulated by the cables that originate from the arches and support the deck of the bridge, are allocated to pedestrian use, resembling the balcony of Palladio's sixteenth-century bridge in Bassano (fig. 1.9). The inclined arches of the Felipe II Bridge extend beyond its deck to reach an underpass for trains. Four stairways, following the extensions of the inclined arches, connect the balconies with the underpass for pedestrian use. Finally, the access ramps of the bridge are architecturally integrated into the main span and supported by piers in the shape of raindrops.

The Felipe II Bridge was Calatrava's first major commission after numerous competitions, sculptures, and commissions in the early to mid-1980s for specific components of buildings. Among those commissions were the design of

Fig. 1.8 | The Felipe II Bridge in Barcelona (1985–1987). Photo by Paolo Rosselli.

a canopy at the entrance of the high school in Wohlen, Switzerland (fig. 1.10), as well as roofs for the library and the main auditorium and a dome for a large central space. He had also designed the facades and doors of the Ernstings Warehouse in Coesfeld, Germany (fig. 1.11). At that time, Calatrava was also actively involved in the design of the Stadelhofen train station in Zurich (fig. 1.12), though neither the expressive structures along its sloping landscape nor the pedestrian bridges had been completed at the time of the Alamillo Bridge commission.

Fig. 1.9	Palladio's bridge in Bassano, northern Italy (original design of 1569, last reconstructed in 1947).
Fig. 1.10	The canopy at the Wohlen High School, Wohlen, Switzerland (1984–1988). Photo by Paolo Rosselli.

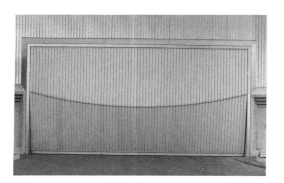

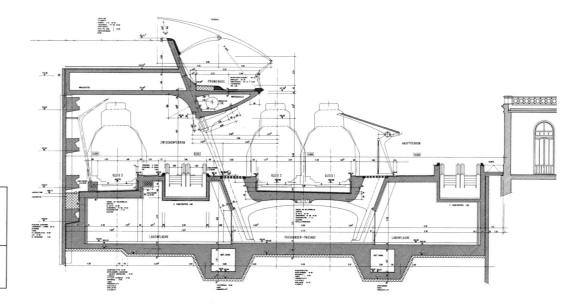

Fig. 1.11	The facade of the Ernstings Ware-house, Coesfeld, Germany (1983–1985). Photo by Paolo Rosselli.
Fig. 1.12	A section of the Stadelhofen train station, Zurich (1983–1990).

Given the importance of the Alamillo Bridge for Expo '92 and the deadline of April 20, 1992, for the opening of the exhibition, Calatrava was requested to work together with a large Spanish engineering firm with experience in large-scale bridge design. After negotiations, Calatrava was paired with the engineering firm Intecsa. Intecsa would undertake the detailed engineering calculations and produce the construction drawings, while Calatrava's office would concentrate on the conceptual design and the engineering design of the most complicated elements. Intecsa was part of the same group of companies as Dragados y Construcciones SA, the largest construction firm in Spain.[2] Based in Madrid, Intecsa had long experience with bridge design both nationally and internationally.

1.2
THE FIRST DESIGN CONCEPT

In the past, the Guadalquivir river had caused several floods in Seville, and its main course was redirected in the late 1970s to pass further west. The flow at the old course of the river, closer to the city, called Meandro de San Jerónimo, was controlled to avoid flooding in the future. Cartuja Island, named after a monastery located on it, was artificially created by the diversion of the Guadalquivir river; it

was on this island that the facilities for Expo '92 were situated.

The Junta of Andalucía solicited the design of a bridge north of the city's center, next to the neighborhood of San Lázaro, to span the shallow and controlled Meandro de San Jerónimo and connect Seville with Cartuja Island. The site did not pose any significant engineering challenges for such a bridge. The river banks were well defined, and the roadway ran perpendicular to the course of the river. The anticipated volume of traffic at the peak of Expo '92 would require three vehicular lanes in each direction. The clear span of the bridge was planned to be on the order of 200 meters, since the construction of piers in the Meandro de San Jerónimo was prohibited, in memory of the forceful flow of the Guadalquivir before its diversion. Furthermore, both banks of the river had a strong bedrock consisting of marl which would easily support the foundations of a 200-meter-long bridge. At that time, no other public facilities were planned in the vicinity of the bridge.

The symmetry of the site and the requirement for a 200-meter span suggested an arched bridge, to be supported uniformly at the two river banks. The Barqueta and El Cachorro bridges constructed at the same time, adjacent to the Alamillo Bridge and with similar site conditions, were de-

signed as variations of arches. The Cartuja Bridge, with a clear span of 170 meters, used box beams as its main structural elements.

Calatrava, in search of a design breakthrough, was not guided by the symmetry of the river banks. Instead, he considered the larger symmetry of the site between the two courses of the river surrounding Cartuja Island and proposed building an "extra-urban viaduct with two river crossings." His intervention would have expanded the scope of the project and introduced two mirror-image bridges, one spanning the Meandro de San Jerónimo and the other spanning the new course of the Guadalquivir (fig. 1.13). The consideration of the symmetry of the larger site led to an asymmetrical bridge over each river. Those bridges, 1.5 kilometers apart, were to be inclined toward the island, creating a symbolic gateway north of the Expo '92 area and a major intervention in the urban design of the island. Furthermore, Calatrava intended to make the urban Alamillo Bridge part of the neighborhood by creating inviting spaces for recreation.

2 Among its other projects, Dragados y Construcciones SA was building the new Seville airport terminal (1989–1991), designed by Rafael Moneo, and several pavilions for Expo '92.

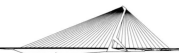

Fig. 1.13 | The master plan of the first design concept for the Alamillo Bridge.

In addition to the two symmetrical bridges, an 876-meter-long elevated viaduct over Cartuja Island was part of the scheme, connecting the two bridges (figs. 1.13, 1.14). The viaduct was integrated architecturally with the bridges and constituted an urban design approach to developing the area and creating monumental architecture. The roadway on the viaduct was kept at the same level as the roadway of the bridges, while the covered pedestrian walkways were positioned on both sides

of the viaduct to ensure proximity to the orange trees on Cartuja Island and the area of Expo '92 (fig. 1.15).

The Ministry of Public Works and Urbanism (MOPU, later renamed Ministry of Public Works and Transport) had jurisdiction over the design and construction of the second bridge over the Guadalquivir river. After Calatrava's proposal, MOPU joined the venture and agreed to have the bridge on the other side of the island designed as a mirror

image of the bridge on the Seville side. That other bridge would be slightly longer and, in order to maintain the same proportions, taller as well. MOPU, however, was reluctant to fully endorse the project, citing issues of technical feasibility and cost.

Initially, each bridge was designed as cable-stayed with a single pylon on the side of the island (fig. 1.16). The shape of that single pylon came out of Calatrava's design vocabulary, as seen in his

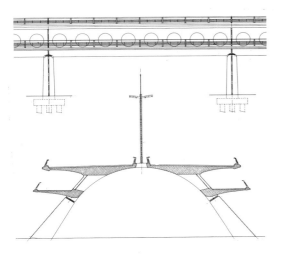

Fig. 1.14	The early drawings for the Cartuja viaduct, elevation and cross section.
Fig. 1.15	The model of the viaduct, located between the two bridges. Photo by Heinrich Helfenstein.
Fig. 1.16	The first design concept for two bridges and a viaduct: site plan.

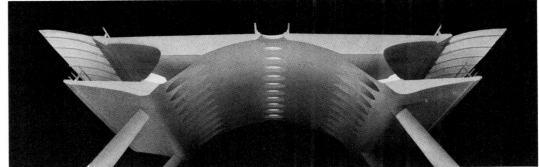

Fig. 1.17	Calatrava's chairs and table designed for the Tabourettli cabaret in Basel (1987), reminiscent of the first design concept for the bridge's pylon. Photo by Paolo Rosselli.
Fig. 1.18	The Montjuïch communications tower for the Olympic Games in Barcelona, designed by Calatrava (1991–1992). Photo by Paolo Rosselli.

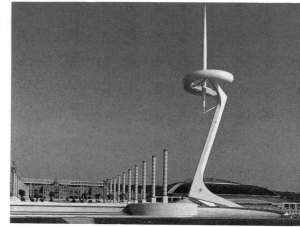

furniture and light fixtures (fig. 1.17). The bridge project marked an early attempt by Calatrava to introduce a shape from his furniture design to a large-scale architectural object. Three years later, in 1991, the Montjuïch communications tower for the Olympic Games in Barcelona was the first realized project to embody such a design (fig. 1.18).

All the cables of the Alamillo Bridge were designed originally to be anchored on the top of the pylon and to support the deck at both sides. Behind the pylon, the roadway was to be aligned with the viaduct. The stabilizing cables on the back of the pylon were to be anchored to the ground.

This scheme was received enthusiastically by the clients, and the partnership between Calatrava and Intecsa was established formally. However, it soon became clear that the innovative pylon would have to be modified.

1.3
TOWARD THE CONSTRUCTED DESIGN

The anchoring of 20 pairs of cables in a small area on the tip of the pylon was technically prohibitive because of the limited available space (fig. 1.16). The inclination of the tip of the pylon also created a geometric difficulty in connecting the backstays,

leading to excessive bending moments. The modifications of the design thus focused on the pylon.

Calatrava studied several schemes for the pylon. All his solutions presumed an asymmetrical bridge on either side of Cartuja Island, with a single pylon on the island bank of the river. Following a series of designs drawn from Calatrava's own vocabulary of compression elements, the proposal for a straight inclined pylon emerged.

The cable stays for the single pylon were now designed to be parallel, anchored in pairs at equal distances along the length of the pylon and supporting the deck along its center axis. A box in the center of the deck provided the deck's neces-

Fig. 1.19 | The Lusitania Bridge, Mérida, Spain, by Calatrava (1988–1992).

sary torsional strength. The cables supported that box in pairs, creating a space for the pedestrian walkway on the top surface of the box, with the roadway cantilevered on both sides. The cantilever resembled that of the Lusitania Bridge in Mérida, Spain (fig. 1.19), which was constructed for the Junta de Extremadura as a design-built project by Calatrava and the construction firm Construcciones y Contratas SA. (This firm later merged with Fomento SA, one of the two contractors for the Alamillo Bridge, to form Fomento de Construcciones y Contratas SA.) Both the pylon and the deck in the first design concept for the Alamillo Bridge were to be constructed in concrete. Behind the py-

lon, the roadway was to touch ground a short distance before the beginning of the viaduct.

Four backstays were considered to support the top of the pylon, lying outside the plane of the bridge and anchored in the landscaped area behind the pylon (fig. 1.20). In that design, however, the location of the cables on the pylon was not optimal. The cables for the deck would load the pylon along its length, while the stabilizing cables would support the pylon at the top only. Thus, the pylon would develop significant bending moments. On the other hand, a large number of parallel backstays anchored along the length of the pylon would make the bridge look like any other cable-stayed

bridge and would alter the space between the bridge and the viaduct.

The next step was to eliminate completely the four backstays, and Calatrava investigated the feasibility of such a design. With the elimination of the backstays, the inclined pylon would rely on its own dead weight, serving as a counterbalance to support the deck of the bridge. In addition, a moment connection at the foundation of the pylon would be necessary to withstand the changing loads on the bridge. The unsupported inclined pylon appeared feasible, though it required engineering fine-tuning and a high precision in construction. Studies showed that the design concept

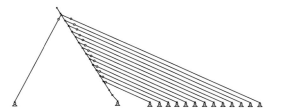 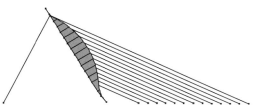 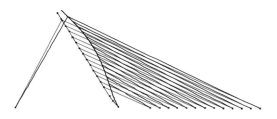

Fig. 1.20 | The straight inclined pylon with backstays at the top, illustrating the projected bending moments and its deflection.

required a lightweight deck and a heavy pylon. Thus, a steel deck was considered for the first time, while the pylon would be constructed of massive concrete in order to increase its weight. Further studies revealed that the compressive forces in the deck, close to the pylon, would require additional compressive strength, possibly to be provided by placing concrete inside the steel deck.

The single pylon springing from the middle of the deck meant that the roadway would be diverted around the pylon, with reversing curves (fig. 1.21). The classification of the road called for traffic speeds of 60 kilometers per hour, which re-

quired an absolute minimum radius of 200 meters for each of the resulting curves. The diversion of the roadway thus created a space behind the pylon of each bridge (fig. 1.22), almost 200 meters long and 70 meters wide, which was used by the designer to introduce public parks. Those parks were to be properly landscaped to create areas for relaxation between the crossings of the rivers and the long viaduct.

The roadway around the pylon of the bridge on the Seville side of the island passed through a site known as the Mirador, which had to be leveled. The Mirador, a small, historic hill 22 meters above the water level at the bank of the Meandro de San Jerónimo, overlooked Seville and was visited often by the public. Initially the engineers of the Junta were hesitant to level the Mirador, but they became convinced that the presence of the bridge would dominate the area such that the Mirador would be

overshadowed. The pedestrian level of the bridge was expected to be approximately 16 meters above the water level, only a few meters below the top of the Mirador, and it would offer wonderful vistas of the city of Seville along the entire length of the bridge.[3]

Calatrava presented the design with the unsupported inclined pylons to the Junta de Anda-

3   During the design stage, there were numerous public discussions about building a public observatory or even a restaurant on the top of the inclined pylon. At a height much taller than the city's Giralda landmark, this observatory, it was thought, would provide glorious views of Seville and the Expo '92 area. The motivation was to make the bridge even more inhabited, to attract more people to visit and explore it. These proposals were never realized, although until the very end a sponsor was sought for the construction of a passenger elevator to run along the back of the pylon.

Fig. 1.21 | The design of the rotaries.

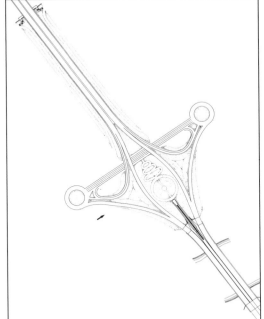

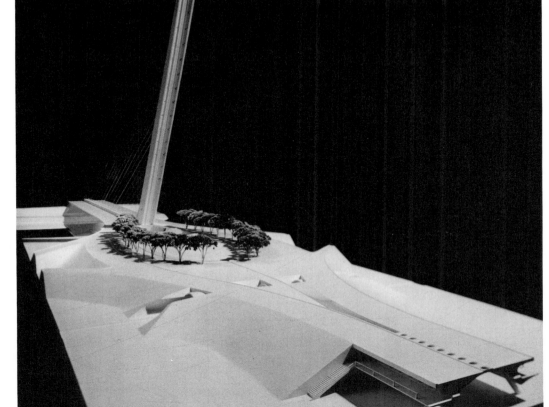

Fig. 1.22 | The park behind the pylon, shown on the model. Photo by Heinrich Helfenstein.

lucía in the summer of 1988, as a replacement of the original design that had won him the commission of the bridge (fig. 1.23). Jaime Montaner, the Commissioner of Public Works of the Junta de Andalucía, was quite excited with the innovations. He immediately realized the importance of such a bridge to the city of Seville, both as a symbol and as a technological wonder, and he supported proceeding with the design development. In September 1988, at the beginning of the design development, Intecsa, Calatrava's technical partner, was not entirely convinced of the technical merits of the proposed solution, but they were willing to explore it further and were committed to making it work, even with the required modifications.

In August 1989, the complexities of the design and the projections for increased costs caused MOPU to drop the design for the second bridge on the other side of Cartuja Island. MOPU decided to adopt a conventional bridge design instead, a bridge with beams supported on piers in the river, as there was nothing to prohibit the construction of piers in that part of the river.

Needless to say, MOPU's decision altered Calatrava's original design concept of a pair of bridges on either side of the Cartuja and an enormous entry to the north of the Expo '92 area. Despite the loss of the intended symmetry, the Junta de Andalucía never wavered in its commitment to Calatrava's design of their part of the scheme, and proceeded with the building of a single bridge on the Seville side, including a 350-meter-long landscaped park and a 526-meter viaduct over the island.

The elimination of the second bridge only served to strengthen the design. The power of the Alamillo Bridge comes from the asymmetry between its two abutments. A mirror image of the Alamillo Bridge on the other side of the island naturally would have restored symmetry to the overall design. The project as built emphasizes the absence of symmetry, which is quite unusual for a bridge of that size. Together with the inclined pylon, the cantilevering roadways, and the elevated walkway, the absence of symmetry challenges the established notion of bridges, making the observer wonder, "What is a bridge?"

Fig. 1.23 | The model of the revised design, showing the two bridges and the viaduct between them. Photo by Heinrich Helfenstein.

2 THE ARCHITECTURE OF THE BRIDGE

Traditionally, bridge design has been practiced within the field of engineering, ruled by technological considerations. Calatrava, in the design of the Alamillo Bridge, moved beyond basic technology to address urban, aesthetic, historic, and symbolic issues as integral components of his design. With regard to the urban setting, the innovations are found in the long sequence of the bridges and the viaduct, the extensive landscaped area at the back of the pylon, and the development of the space under the bridges. On the cable-stayed bridge on the Seville side, Calatrava's innovations appear in the inclined self-standing pylon, the design of the cross section of the deck, the pedestrian walkway, the railings and safety barriers, and the illumination. Dominated by ambitious engineering in the service of design, this bridge displays an architectural sensitivity unlike the large majority of bridges.

2.1
ARCHITECTURE AND BRIDGES

An architectural discussion of the Alamillo Bridge should start by exploring the relation between architecture and bridges. The historical meaning of architecture—the design of artifacts to be built by a team following the directions of a single leader—applies to bridges as well. The emphasis is on tectonics for a general class of constructions beyond only those that enclose space. Architecture uses a certain class of materials for those constructions, such as stone, brick, steel, concrete, wood, glass. These materials have common properties: they are heavy, are produced inexpensively in large quantities, and withstand time and the elements of nature. Over time, however, architecture has become associated with the creation of shelters for human activities, focusing primarily on buildings. Architecture thus goes beyond tectonics and addresses issues of space and its use, referring to the social sciences as well as to precedent and historic context.

In the last fifteen years, there has emerged a synergy of architecture and engineering in the design of a few very distinctive bridges, such as the Alamillo Bridge. Typically, the program requirements for these bridges do not pose complicated engineering problems; instead, the bridge designs are based on expressing architectural intentions. Several examples of this new bridge design are found in Europe, mostly as a result of design competitions or direct commissions to architects.

This synergy of architecture and engineering brings new values to the design of bridges. Efficiency and effectiveness are no longer the only aims; architectural considerations have begun to emphasize the importance of historical associations, symbolism, form, space, context, and cultural meaning. Thus, the former dry approach of abstract mathematical models and concepts gives way to a more integrated and human approach to bridge design. On the other hand, the physical form of a bridge continues to be shaped directly from the type and form of the structural system, which is exposed and predominant. Bridges have neither skin nor absolutely enclosed spaces to hide their structural system. In addition, the construction process often imposes engineering problems of a magnitude similar to those of the structural behavior of the completed bridge. A deep understanding of the behavior of structural systems and the materials employed is essential to designing a bridge.

Such demanding requirements lead naturally to a team approach to design. Part of the team contributes the engineering skills and construction expertise and part of the team contributes the architecturally bound design vision. However, the respective contributions are rarely weighed equally. Since the engineering team contributes the technological expertise that dominates the design of a bridge, it has more control in the design process, leaving the architectural designer with marginal, often ornamental, responsibilities. In the few bridges that represent exceptions to this rule, it is clear that either the engineering designer had a direct interest in the architecture of the bridge, or a single person assumed both the design and the analytical responsibilities (Menn, 1991).

The control of both the design and the analytical responsibilities by a single principal designer is facilitated greatly by a maturing structural and construction technology. A variety of structural schemes and available materials have been studied extensively for a wide spectrum of problems, and their behavior is by now well understood. As a result, design interventions move the program beyond the immediate boundaries of function and efficiency to explore other avenues for design expression. These interventions effect a shift from decisions made on the basis of pure engineering toward the architectural domain, with distinct implications for overall design.

The Alamillo Bridge exemplifies this shift. A single principal designer, Santiago Calatrava, with expertise in both architecture and engineering, was in charge of the conceptual design. He applied architectural intentions that transformed the relatively conventional design problem of a 200-meter-long bridge into the realization of a monumental bridge on the frontiers of today's technology.

2.2
TECHNOLOGY IN THE DESIGN OF THE ALAMILLO BRIDGE

The architecture of bridges, like any other construction activity, is governed by technology. Based on the working definition that *design is a means of inquiry to impose meaningful order,* it can be proposed that *technology is the means available to impose meaningful order* (Pollalis and Bakos, 1996). In that context, technology can be seen both as an enabler and as a constraint in the design process. A particular technology enables the transformation of available resources into design goals. Thus, while design addresses "what," technology addresses "how."

Technology, among other things, establishes the *resources-benefits* characteristics of bridge building. Here these terms do not necessarily reflect monetary sums, but they acknowledge that during the design process there is a transformation of inputs to outputs, and that the technology employed determines both the efficiency and the qualitative aspects of that transformative process. The excess engineering of the Alamillo Bridge, reflecting a deliberate choice to produce monumental architecture rather than an inconspicuous river crossing, deviated from the established transformation of inputs to outputs for the 200-meter span. It is commonly understood that the resources required for a bridge always depend on its span length. However, the transformation of inputs to outputs depends on the desired output. In the Alamillo Bridge, the available technology determined the required inputs for the implementation of the vision of the designer.

In addition to establishing the resources-benefits characteristics, technology establishes frontiers of feasibility, setting limits that cannot be exceeded regardless of the available resources. Available technology determines what can and what cannot be done. The cost-benefit characteristics of existing technology deteriorate significantly as these limits are reached.

It was the selected design and not the site that set the Alamillo Bridge at the frontiers of feasibility: most of the technological challenges could have been avoided if a conventional design had been chosen, like the designs of the other bridges a few hundred meters down the river (see figs. 1.3, 1.4, 1.5). After the specific design was selected, however, technological limitations governed to a great extent the design development and the building of the bridge. The design of the foundation, the required precision in construction for the equilibrium of the bridge, the length of the cables, and the pumping of concrete were among the elements of the bridge that challenged the limits of technological feasibility. As a result of approaching those limits, the resources required to build the bridge increased disproportionately to its span length. Technology in the Alamillo Bridge was not brought in just as an architectural expression or style, as in Piano and Rogers's Pompidou Center or Norman Foster's Hong Kong and Shanghai Bank. The technological obstacles were real and pressing, and required intense engineering efforts to be resolved.

Looking at the matter from a different perspective, one could say that the design of bridges employs mature *low technology,* with time-resistant materials and proven construction techniques—in contrast to *high technology,* which describes a rapidly changing technology with major advances in its cost-benefit characteristics and its feasibility frontier. Bridges should operate continuously for a long time, without frequent service periods that require closing them. These requirements of a long life expectancy and continuous operation restrict the applicability of complex and sophisticated technical solutions that require extensive maintenance and have a higher probability of failure. Coupled with traditional construction processes that pay little attention to future flexibility in use and maintenance, these requirements lead to conservative, low-technology construction solutions for most bridges.

It is the mature low technology of bridges that allowed Calatrava to develop his formal design intentions for the Alamillo Bridge by introducing constraints internal to the design process, constraints subjective rather than objective in nature. The design of the single, unsupported inclined pylon was the result of strong design intentions not immediately related to the use of the bridge, the available technology for the size of the bridge, or the available resources. The intention of the designer focused on the creation of a bold object to attract curiosity and even cause anxiety in the spectator. Short and medium-length bridges, requiring a technology that is mature and widely available, are the prime candidates for designs based on such artistic considerations, whereas longer bridges are designed predominantly on technological grounds. The development of internal subjective constraints tends to make bridge design, for a wide spectrum of span lengths, comparable to high-technology disciplines and helps to hide a bridge's underlying low technology.

The technological challenges in building the Alamillo Bridge can be compared only to much longer bridges built in more difficult sites. Calatrava's inspiration to build a cable-stayed bridge with a single unsupported pylon made the construction of the bridge quite groundbreaking, comparable to the building of the Brooklyn Bridge in the nineteenth century, or to celebrated bridges at sites with major natural obstacles, such as the Golden Gate Bridge or the George Washington Bridge.

2.3
CALATRAVA'S VISUAL VOCABULARY: SCULPTURES AND BRIDGES

The shaping of the form often links sculpture with architecture. Sculpture is the art of giving form and shape to materials. Sculptures and buildings draw from the same materials, such as marble, stone, steel, wood, and glass. Sculptures, however, unlike buildings, are not grounded in immediate function, do not enclose controlled space, and are smaller in scope and size. Buildings can notably incorporate elements of sculpture, often in the form of shaped elements or assemblies of elements. In fact, every element of a building can be treated as a piece of sculpture. The synthesis of those elements creates space, which is the higher purpose of architecture. Furthermore, sculpture does not inherently require a team effort, and there is no need to distinguish between the design and its implementation, or between the sculptor in command and others involved in the process.

Calatrava has designed sculptures since his early years as a designer (figs. 2.1, 2.2). They serve as models for his explorations of shapes, forces, and equilibrium. Most of them include massive elements in compression and thin wires in tension. The elements in compression are bold, with generous dimensions and excess weight. They are made of a variety of materials such as wood, bronze, steel, granite, marble, or stone. The wires are emphatically thin, made exclusively from stainless steel. The connections between the tension and compression elements, and between the elements and their foundations, are stressed visually by in-

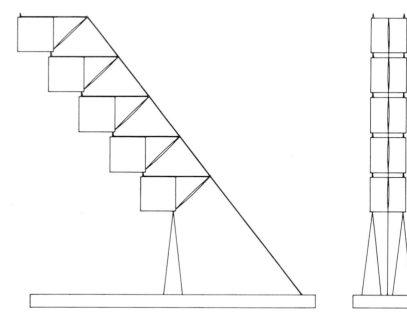

corporating elaborate details where the elements touch each other on sharp and pointed edges.

Calatrava's sculptural assemblies have different configurations, but all have the explicit intention of puzzling the observer. The first puzzle results from the disproportionate sizes of the tensile and the compressive elements. While the highest-strength wires are used for the tensile elements, resulting in extremely thin sections, the compressive elements are overemphasized, taking massive forms. The observer is overwhelmed with the mass of the compressive elements and pays less attention to the visually minimal tensile elements, which provokes questions about the structure's stability. The second puzzle is generated by questions of gravity, of how the sculpture stays in place. This visual game is played mostly by the location of the thin supporting wires. Often the foundation provides the necessary support by developing a moment connection, always as a result of a couple of forces. The tensile force of the foundation is always applied on a wire, while the compressive force acts on the much larger area of a compression element.

Like Calatrava's sculptures, the Alamillo Bridge puzzles the observer with regard to its stability. This bridge was the first of his works to neglect issues of scale, transferring a design from the scale of sculpture and furniture to a full-scale work of architecture. In the superstructure of a bridge, however, it is much more difficult to control precisely the weight and the exact position of the different elements than in a sculpture. Likewise, the varying loading conditions make the transition from the equilibrium of a sculpture to the equilibrium of a full-scale bridge quite challenging. Variations in the estimated weights of either the pylon or the deck could cause major deviations in the forces and the equilibrium of the bridge. Under dead loads only, an increase in the weight of the pylon of the Alamillo Bridge by 10% could result in an increase of the bending moments at the base of the pylon by 62%, reaching the limits imposed by safety factors. Thus, low tolerances and precision in construction were necessary to build the Alamillo Bridge, in a way that sculptures do not require. In addition, a rigid foundation, while feasible in sculptures, creates problems for a large bridge. The uncertainties in the behavior of the soil and the soil-to-structure interaction led to the design of a massive foundation for the Alamillo Bridge. While some rotation is expected to occur in the foundation, it is designed not to exceed 0.06°.

Fascinated by the concept of high-rise buildings as phallic objects, Calatrava attempted through the pylon to assimilate the same associa-

Fig. 2.2 | Reinforced concrete sculpture (11 meters high) at the Venice Biennale. Photo by Paolo Rosselli.

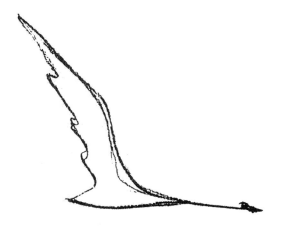

tions to his bridge (fig. 2.3). The design of the rotaries below the inclined pylon enhances the analogy to male sexual organs (see fig. 1.21). Calatrava relies more specifically on the image of a flying bird as his inspiration for the bridge. His own widely published sketch (fig. 2.4), often pictured next to the cable-stayed bridge, suggests that the analogy of a flying bird to a flying pylon or a flying bridge without backstays had been in the designer's mind during the development of the design.

The visual affinity between the bird and the bridge hinges on captured motion. Constantin Brancusi, with sculptures such as *Bird in Space* (fig. 2.5), has had a strong influence on Calatrava's shapes. The visual similarities of some of Calatrava's sculptures (fig. 2.6) to those of Brancusi have been acknowledged by Calatrava himself, while the free forms of the sculptor-artist shift toward more well-defined forms created by the engineer-artist. The increased definition and standardization of forms is evident in the progression from Calatrava's drawings and sculptures of birds to the architectural model for the Alamillo Bridge to the construction of the actual bridge. The pylon of the bridge also has a strong affinity to Brancusi's *Never-Ending Column* (fig. 2.7) as it disappears toward the sky.

Fig. 2.3	The pylon of the bridge as a gigantic phallic object.
Fig. 2.4	Sketch by Calatrava comparing a flying bird to the Alamillo Bridge (1988).

Fig. 2.5	Constantin Brancusi, *Bird in Space* (1928). Museum of Modern Art, New York.
Fig. 2.6	Calatrava's bird sculpture appears four times at both entrances of the 9 d'Octubre Bridge, Valencia (1986–1989).
Fig. 2.7	Constantin Brancusi, *Endless Column* (1918).

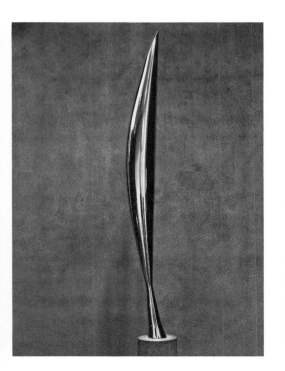

2.4
THE SELECTION OF THE INCLINED PYLON

The Alamillo's single inclined pylon without backstays had no precedent in either bridge design or building design.[1] However, beyond the formal design intentions, the concept of the inclined pylon has an inherent engineering logic.

Most cable-stayed bridges support two spans of similar length on either side of the pylon, an optimal arrangement for a double-cantilevered structure. In an effort to avoid bending moments on the pylon in such bridges, the free cantilevering span is slightly longer, while the last cable of the back span is anchored on the ground. Under the bridge's own weight and the live load on the free cantilevering span only, the backstays are loaded further (fig. 2.8). If the live load is on the back span only, then it is in equilibrium with the longer and heavier free span. The anchored backstays provide equilibrium even for spans with a significant difference between the longer free span and the shorter back span. So the pylons for most cable-stayed bridges are subject to axial loads only and do not develop bending moments even for unbalanced loading between the free span and the back span.

There are certain situations in which backstays cannot be anchored, such as within a series of cable-stayed bridges positioned in a row to span long distances. If the cables are not anchored to the ground, the spans should be equal so that there is no unbalanced dead load, and the pylon must carry the bending moments resulting from any unbalanced live or wind load. If the spans are not equal on the two sides of the pylon, the shorter span needs to be heavier in order to achieve equilibrium. If w_{long} is the distributed load on the long span and w_{short} the distributed load on the short span, and L_{long} and L_{short} the respective lengths of those spans, then for a moment equilibrium:

$$\frac{1}{2}w_{long} \times L_{long}^2 = \frac{1}{2}w_{short} \times L_{short}^2 \rightarrow$$

$$\frac{w_{short}}{w_{long}} = \left(\frac{L_{long}}{L_{short}}\right)^2 \qquad (2.1)$$

Such a ratio is quite difficult to achieve for spans with a substantial difference in length.

Fig. 2.9 shows the relationship of point loads so that there is no bending moment at the base of the pylon (i.e., so that there is no horizontal component to the load at the top of the pylon). If the back span cannot provide the necessary weight, then anchoring is required.

An inclined pylon skewed toward the shorter span (fig. 2.10) could improve the distribution of forces in a cable-stayed bridge with uneven spans, although the reactions at the supports will remain the same as in a similar bridge with a vertical pylon (fig. 2.9). An inclined pylon significantly reduces the tension in the backstays, as well as the compression in the back span. At the same time, there is a modest increase in the compressive force in the pylon. However, the greatest gain comes from a reduction of the components of the forces acting perpendicular to the axis of the pylon from the cable stays. Although those forces are in equilibrium, the pylon deforms before it reaches such an equilibrium. Forces of a smaller magnitude imply a smaller deformation, which is preferable for a pylon that is quite rigid, and a certain moment connection at its base is always required.

There are several examples of inclined pylons in the design of cable-stayed structures. Pier

1 Two inclined apartment towers in Madrid, leaning toward each other to create a gateway over the Avenida Castellana, were designed and their construction started after that of the Alamillo Bridge. These apartment towers are supported on massive foundations, without any exterior cables; but interior cables strengthen the tension zone of the towers.

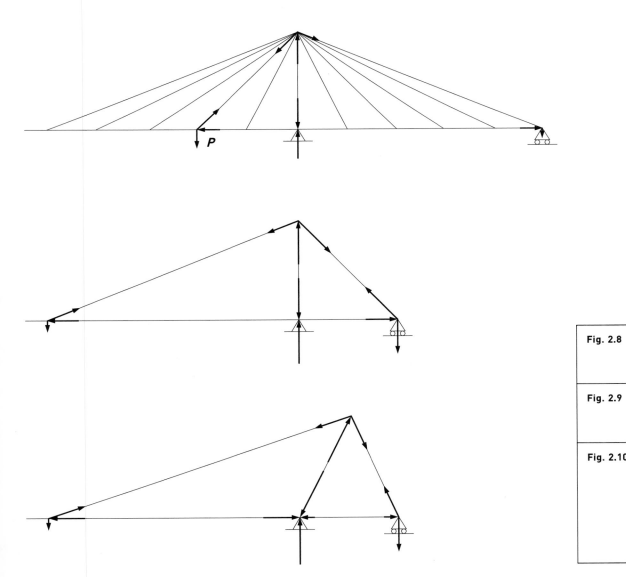

Fig. **2.8**	Asymmetrical live load *P* on a typical cable-stayed bridge with two spans of similar length.
Fig. **2.9**	The equilibrium of a cable-stayed bridge with unequal spans and a vertical pylon.
Fig. **2.10**	The backstays of a cable-stayed bridge with an inclined pylon take a smaller force than for a similar bridge with a vertical pylon, while the components of the forces from the cables acting perpendicular to the pylon are reduced.

| Fig. 2.11 | Pier Luigi Nervi, Burgo paper mill, Mantua, Italy (1961–1962). |
| Fig. 2.12 | Josef Lacko-Aprad, Bridge of the Slovak National Uprising, Bratislava, Slovakia, with a restaurant on top of the pylon (1966–1973). |

Luigi Nervi inclined the pylons that support the suspended roof of the Burgo paper mill in Mantua (fig. 2.11), in an effort to increase the distance between the two pylons and thus to increase the open space within the factory. The 50-meter-tall pylons support a clear center span of 160 meters, with rear cantilevers of 43 meters. Thus, the ratio of free to back span is almost 2:1. Similarly, the Bridge of the Slovak National Uprising in Bratislava over the Danube, designed by Josef Lacko-Aprad, is supported by an inclined pylon (fig. 2.12). A superstructure on the pylon's head, housing a café accessed by elevator through one leg of the pylon, provides additional weight at the top of the pylon, contributing to the equilibrium of the bridge. The longer span of the bridge is 303 meters, while the shorter span at the back of the pylon is 74 meters. The Bratislava bridge is narrower than the Alamillo Bridge and has a stiffer deck, supported by fewer cables. Thus, the clear spans of the deck between cables are 74 meters; the cables support the deck in the middle and are anchored at the pylon's top.

On the Alamillo Bridge, the location of the pylon on the river bank at the island side does not allow the construction of two spans of similar proportions on either side of the pylon, as a long span extending over land (in lieu of the viaduct) would be unnecessary. An inclined pylon would naturally decrease significantly the required length of a span over land and provide a gesture of balanced forces. However, unlike the bridge in Bratislava, the Alamillo Bridge completely eliminates the span at the back of the pylon as well as the cables on that side. The weight of the pylon is the only force counteracting the forces of the cables that support the deck.

2.5
THE DESIGN OF THE CROSS SECTION

The architectural consideration of bridges is too often limited to studying their longitudinal elevation. Longitudinal views of bridges can be had only from a distance, most likely from another bridge or along the river bank. On the other hand, a bridge's cross section communicates the most significant understanding of the bridge, both for pedestrians and for the passengers in crossing vehicles. Furthermore, it is the design of the cross section that creates space and produces a three-dimensional object.

The selection of a single unsupported pylon for the Alamillo Bridge forced the cable stays to be anchored in the pylon at equal distances. The cable stays also required anchoring in the middle of the deck, in order to maintain the required clearance for vehicular traffic. Thus, the cables were designed to be anchored on a box located in the middle of the deck, running along the length of the bridge. As in several similar designs, that box needed to be supported by the cable stays for vertical loads, while itself providing the necessary torsional support for asymmetrical live loads acting on the roadway.

The cross section of the Alamillo Bridge is similar to that of the Lusitania Bridge in Mérida (fig. 2.13), which Calatrava designed during the same time period. However, the torsion box and the cantilevering ribs of the Lusitania Bridge are made of concrete. Both bridges are reminiscent in cross section of the shape of the unbuilt monolithic Butterfly Bridge over the Ohio River by Frank Lloyd Wright (fig. 2.14).

There are several precedents for the engineering design of such a cross section. One is the Raiffeisen cable-stayed bridge on the Rhine in Germany, close to Neuwied, designed by Bung, Homberg, Grossi, Leonhardt and Andrä (figs. 2.15, 2.16). The cross section of that bridge is supported by cables in the middle, on a steel torsion box.[2] Steel girders cantilever from the box to support six lanes of traffic, three on each side. The bridge has clear spans of 235 and 212 meters on either side of the pylon; the pylon itself, in an A form, encloses a deck span of 38.4 meters. The width of the bridge is 35.5 meters, while the pylon stands 89 meters above the roadway. Pedestrian walkways are located on each edge of the deck, toward the end of the cantilevers. The walkways are at the same level as the roadway, which induces the pedestrians to feel both the large size of the bridge and the intensity of the vehicular traffic. The cantilevers are visually integrated into the torsion box, making the deck look architecturally like a solid element.

On both the Alamillo and Lusitania bridges, contrariwise, the pedestrians are completely separated from vehicular traffic. They walk on top of the torsion box, among the cables. The cables create a protected space that transforms as the pedestrians walk closer to the pylon. On the Alamillo Bridge, the elevation of the walkway 1.8 meters above the roadway gives a more comfortable feeling to the pedestrians, reminiscent of the separation between pedestrians and traffic on the Brooklyn Bridge

2   "Steel box" and "torsion box" are used interchangeably in the text. Although "torsion box" characterizes a unique function for the center steel box along the middle of the deck of the bridge, that box also serves as a beam in bending and shearing.

Fig. 2.13 | Cross section of the Lusitania Bridge, Mérida.

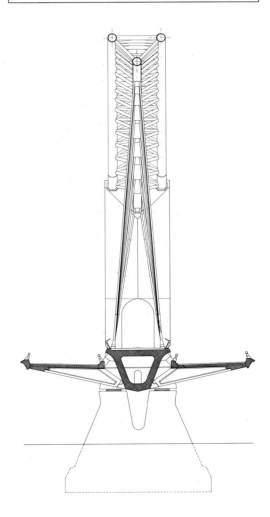

Fig. 2.15 | The single-pylon Raiffeisen cable-stayed bridge on the Rhine (1974–1979).

Fig. 2.16 | The structure of the deck of the Raiffeisen Bridge.

(figs. 2.17, 2.18). There, vehicles use the lower deck and pedestrians are elevated to the upper deck, which they occupy exclusively. Furthermore, the two middle cables of the four main suspension cables define the boundaries of the walkway and create a protective space. The timber floor gives a human dimension to the walkway and makes the passage along the bridge quite pleasant. The size of the Brooklyn Bridge also allows the positioning of decorative light fixtures and benches along the walkway (for which the Alamillo lacks the space).

The two cantilevered roadways of the Alamillo Bridge are also separated horizontally from the torsion box by openings that allow light to pass through the bridge deck, as in Calatrava's designs for the 9 d'Octubre Bridge in Valencia (fig. 2.19) and the unrealized Wettstein Bridge for Basel (fig. 2.20). The space under the Alamillo Bridge was a primary concern in the design of the bridge. The purity of the lines under the bridge receives the same attention as the elements on the top of the bridge. The steel wings of the cantilever, located every 4 meters, are clearly defined, and the torsion box is the only longitudinal element under the bridge. Both roadways are presented as one-way slabs, supported on the wings, making them look lighter and distinguishing them from the two-level structural skeleton of the box and the wings.

The openings between the torsion box and the two roadways separate the bridge into three different parts, interrupting the continuity of the mass. However, there is a price for the separation of the masses: the steel box is by necessity smaller than a steel box that would structurally incorporate part of the deck. Thus, thicker steel plates are needed to withstand the developed torsion, while the deck is less aerodynamic in serving as a down-lifting foil for lateral wind. The design separation of the masses of the center box and the cantilevering roadways transforms the roadways into structurally inactive cantilevers that take the vertical live loads only.

The resemblance of the deck to an organic skeleton is evident, recalling Calatrava's frequent references to animal skeletons (fig. 2.21). The box of the bridge represents the spine, while the wings are like the ribs springing from the spine. The physical separation between the box and the road-

| **Fig. 2.17** | The walkway on the Brooklyn Bridge (1869–1883). |
| **Fig. 2.18** | The walkway on the Alamillo Bridge, showing a striking affinity to the Brooklyn Bridge. |

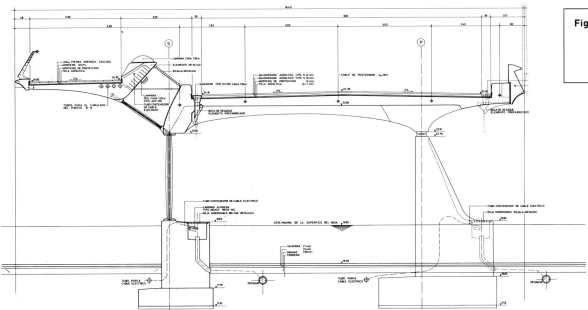

Fig. 2.19 | A cross section of the 9 d'Octubre Bridge, Valencia, showing the horizontal separation between pedestrians and vehicular traffic.

Fig. 2.20 | A cross section of the Wettstein Bridge, Basel (unbuilt project, 1988), showing the horizontal separation between pedestrians and vehicular traffic.

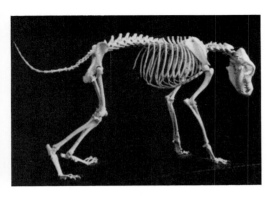

Fig. 2.21 | The skeleton of Calatrava's own dog (1983). Photo by Heinrich Helfenstein.

ways enhances the idea of an elastic and moving connection between the spine and the ribs. Comparisons to earlier designs of cable-stayed bridges with centrally located cables and cantilevering decks reveal the strong design of the Alamillo Bridge with its pure lines. Most bridges designed with engineering efficiency often yield quite complex forms that can be read only within a dry engineering vocabulary. The Alamillo Bridge projects simplicity.

During the development of the construction drawings, several details had to be redesigned in order to make them easier to produce, and several details were simplified for construction (as will be discussed in chapter 6). However, such simplifications were guided always by the contractor's commitment to make a bridge as close to the intentions of the designer as possible.

2.6
LIGHTS, SAFETY BARRIERS, TRAFFIC SIGNS

The bridge was designed with great attention to details and an absolute commitment to design perfection. The particular form of every element and detail was designed with the same attention as the individual pieces of a larger sculpture. Thus, standard lighting fixtures and safety barriers used in highways and other bridges could not be placed on that bridge.

However, there are inherent difficulties in the design of secondary elements, such as lighting fixtures, safety barriers, and traffic signs, and their integration within the scheme of a bridge. Regulatory agencies dictate their design to meet strict safety specifications, and they require extensive testing. Standardized designs are driven by function and performance, while aesthetic considerations assume a secondary role. The Felipe II Bridge in Barcelona, in its urban setting with low-speed traffic, had set a precedent in integrating the design of safety elements with the rest of the bridge (fig. 2.22). On that bridge, artificial lighting was integrated into custom-designed stainless steel handrails and safety barriers. The Alamillo Bridge, however, is longer than the Felipe II Bridge, and is located in a suburban setting with a higher speed limit of 60 kilometers per hour. The designer made extensive efforts to convince the Junta that standard safety elements would be incompatible with the architecture of the bridge. After long negotiations, the Junta got permission from the national Ministry of Transportation to customize the design of those elements, and Calatrava was allowed to design both the light fixtures and the safety barriers. The latter were designed to resemble the pedestrian handrails and were tested and approved for strength and ductility before production.

Integrated lighting has been a major element in the architecture of Calatrava. His building and bridge designs incorporate artificial lighting from the very early stages of the design process; natural light is designed to reach otherwise dark areas, through skylights and openings in bridges' decks. His image of the light fixtures for the Alamillo Bridge was quite different from traditional lighting on highways. Instead of using tall posts, Calatrava introduced low-level continuous lighting,

in an effort to avoid any vertical elements that would compete with the inclined pylon. The railings, the safety barriers, and the lighting of the Alamillo Bridge have a close affinity to those Wright designed for the unbuilt Butterfly Bridge (fig. 2.23).

Calatrava was less successful in receiving permission to redesign the traffic signs. Initially, he succeeded in convincing the Junta and the Ministry not to place any traffic signs on the bridge, other than the painted lines separating the traffic lanes. Later, however, the Ministry considered that solution unsafe and installed a large traffic sign just before the pylon. That traffic sign alerts westbound drivers to the junction with the road that goes to the site of Expo '92. The large size of the sign, supported on both sides by long posts and spanning the three westbound lanes of the bridge, recalls the standard traffic signs of highways. Both

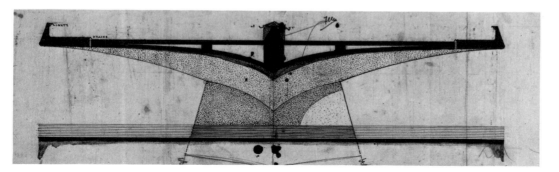

Fig. 2.22	The railings and illumination of the Felipe II Bridge, Barcelona. Photo by Paolo Rosselli.
Fig. 2.23	A cross section of the Butterfly Bridge, showing the railings and the illumination of the bridge. Frank Lloyd Wright Foundation.

the poles and the truss that support it make no effort to accommodate the design intentions of the
bridge, especially in violating Calatrava's determi-
nation to avoid any vertical elements.

2.7
SELECTION OF MATERIALS

In addition to shaping the forms, Calatrava care-
fully chose the materials for the Alamillo Bridge.
The exposed materials are either steel or concrete.
All steel surfaces are painted white, and all exposed
concrete is white concrete. The main cables are
placed inside white polyethylene protective tubes
and the railings and the light fixtures are also
painted white. The stainless steel components for
the railings are the only parts that are not white,
for contrast and to invite pedestrians to touch the
shining material.

The white color smoothly integrates the elements of the bridge and unifies the different con-
stitutions of the various materials. Furthermore, it
denies the materialization of the elements and
gives a unifying purity to the bridge. At the risk of
requiring increased attention and maintenance,
Calatrava has followed the practice of painting
his bridges white ever since his first bridge in
Barcelona.

3   THE ENGINEERING OF THE BRIDGE

The innovative design of the Alamillo Bridge pushed engineering to the frontiers of technology. The technical challenges for structural engineering centered on the stability of the bridge and the strength and stiffness of the pylon and the deck, both under service loads and during construction. Designer-engineer Santiago Calatrava, as well as engineers Carlos Alonso-Cobo of Santander, José Ramón Atienza-Reales of Valencia, and Angel C. Aparicio of Barcelona, successfully faced those challenges; their solutions defined the structural materials and the geometry of the elements of the bridge.

This chapter presents first the conceptual engineering design of the bridge, explaining the hierarchy of its structural members and its static indeterminacy. The preliminary design of the

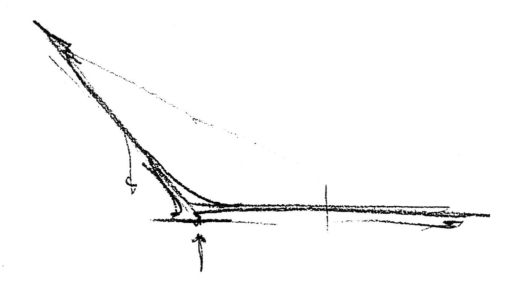

Fig. 3.1 | An early sketch by Calatrava explaining the equilibrium of his proposed design for the Alamillo Bridge.

structural members follows, including the post-tensioning forces in the cable stays. Later, in chapter 4, the finite element model is described, with specific information on its geometry, the mechanical properties of the building materials, the loading cases that were analyzed, and the results obtained.

3.1
THE STRUCTURAL ORDER OF THE BRIDGE

There is a four-level structural hierarchy in the Alamillo Bridge: the live loads apply on the deck and then are transferred to the cables, the pylon, and finally the foundation (fig. 3.1).

3.1.1
THE DECK

The deck of the bridge (fig. 3.2) is composed of a steel box running along the longitudinal axis of the bridge, pairs of cantilevering steel girders on both sides of the hexagonal box, and the concrete slabs that constitute the roadways.

The design intentions called for a visual separation of the concrete deck, the cantilevering steel girders, and the steel box. Such a separation lets each component carry its own forces independently and eliminates any continuous action that would increase the stiffness of the deck. Thus, the concrete slab does not incorporate the cantilevering girders into its structural properties and, even more important, the cantilevering girders do not provide any additional stiffness to the steel box.

The live loads from the vehicular traffic are supported by the concrete slabs of the roadways on both sides of the steel box. Those one-way slabs rest on the cantilevering steel girders every 4 m along the entire length of the bridge. Each pair of steel girders on opposite sides of the deck are connected to each other with a strut inside the steel box, forming a continuous beam across the entire width of the cross section (fig. 3.3). Thus, under a balanced live load on both sides of the roadway, the steel box is subject to a single concentrated force where the steel girders connect to the box. The magnitude of such a concentrated load is determined by the dead and the live loads on the section.

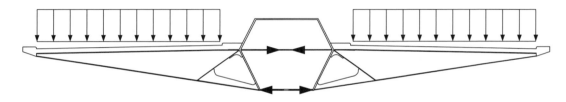

The steel box that constitutes the main structural element along the axis of the deck is supported by the cable stays, the pedestal of the pylon, and the east abutment. The cable stays, located every 12 m, carry axial loads at a 24° angle with the horizontal. Thus, the steel box is a continuous beam with a 171.50 m free span and elastic directional supports every 12 m, subject to a uniform load from the pedestrian live load and its own weight as well as to concentrated forces every 4 m from the steel cantilevers (fig. 3.4). As a continuous beam, the box should be sufficiently stiff at the connections with the cables to transfer the loads across several pairs of cables, and to avoid excessive local deformations (fig. 3.5). Furthermore, the inclination of the cables produces an axial compressive force in the steel box that is transferred to the base of the pylon. Close to the pylon, the magnitude of the compressive force is quite high (fig. 3.6).

For partial live load on one side of the roadway, the bending moments of the two opposite steel girders are not balanced and the steel box is

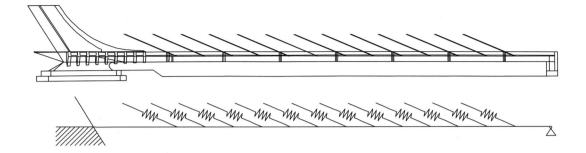

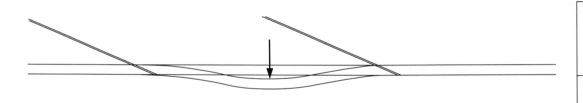

Fig. 3.4	The steel box is a continuous beam with supports at the two abutments and elastic directional supports every 12 m.
Fig. 3.5	The steel box should have sufficient stiffness that it does not experience local deformations as a result of concentrated loads.
Fig. 3.6	An illustration of the axial compressive force in the deck, juxtaposed to the weight of the deck and the forces of the cables. The thickness of the step graph along the deck represents the magnitude of the compressive forces along the deck, on the same scale as the line thickness of the arrows.

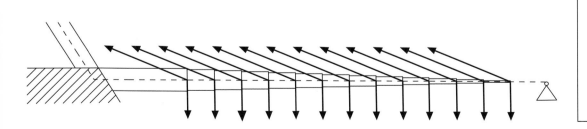

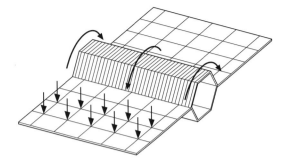

| **Fig. 3.7** | The steel box provides the torsional strength of the cross section. |

loaded with a torsional moment. With less than a 5 m distance between the cables of every pair across the 32 m wide deck, the cable stays cannot take any significant moment by adjusting the axial force in each cable. Thus, the torsional moment resulting from partial live load is withstood by the torsional strength of the steel box, acting as a simply supported beam between the east abutment and the pedestal of the pylon (fig. 3.7).

3.1.2
THE CABLE STAYS

The cables stays transfer the loads from the deck to the pylon. The cables, loaded under their own weight and the pre-tensioning force, take the shape of the catenary and are expected to develop a certain amount of sagging (see fig. 3.19).

3.1.3
THE PYLON

The pylon is loaded from the forces of the cable stays and with its own weight. The resultant of those two forces is inclined and should follow as closely as possible the direction of the pylon (fig. 3.8). However, as the live loads on the deck change, so do the axial forces in the cable stays. Thus, the direction of the resultant force in the pylon changes as well, generating bending moments in the pylon (fig. 3.9). This is quite different from the state of forces expected in the pylons of most cable-stayed bridges, designed with cables supporting the deck on both sides of the pylon and having the end cables anchored in the ground. In those bridges, the pylons are not subject to moments but only to axial forces, as the anchored backstays take the horizontal component of the force transmitted by the cables on the pylon (see fig. 2.8).

The funicular loading, under which the pylon is subject to axial forces only, should correspond to a "middle-ground" loading condition.[1]

Thus, under various loading conditions, the pylon would be subject to reversing bending moments with similar magnitudes; under extreme loading conditions these correspond to either the least load or the largest load. Considering dead and live loads only, the middle-ground loading should correspond to the dead load of the bridge plus half the anticipated maximum live load. With no live load, the forces in the cables would decrease, resulting in negative bending moments for the pylon and a positive moment at the foundation.[2] On the other hand, under a maximum live load on the deck, the cable forces would increase, pulling the pylon and generating positive bending moments for the pylon and a negative moment at the foundation. Since the two extreme loading conditions are generated by antisymmetric live loads, the magnitude of the positive bending moments should be

---

1 The pylon will always experience minor bending moments since its own weight is a distributed load and the forces of the cables are concentrated loads.

2 A positive bending moment on the pylon, or the deck, causes tension at the lower fibers of the elements. A positive moment at a support is a counterclockwise moment. The pylon is assumed to be at the left, i.e., the observer is looking north, like all the structural models presented in this book.

equal to the magnitude of the negative bending moments.

Temperature changes, wind, and earthquakes generate environmental loads which, combined with the dead, permanent, and live loads, dictate the design of the bridge. Environmental loads also act in a direction transverse to the axis of the bridge, requiring strength in the lateral direction and causing deformations that should be considered for second-order effects. Subject to those loads (which will be quantified in chapter 4), the loading condition for the funicular loading of the pylon will not in fact coincide exactly with the dead load plus half the maximum live load on the deck, although this is a good first approximation.

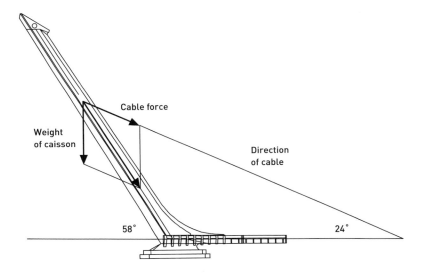

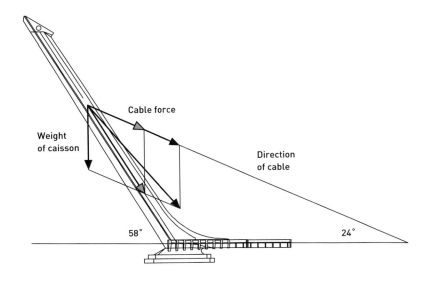

Fig. 3.8	Under funicular loading, the resultant of the axial force in a pair of cables and the weight of the pylon should coincide with the axis of the pylon.
Fig. 3.9	When the axial force in a pair of cables changes, the pylon is subject to bending moments, as the resultant force no longer coincides with the axis of the pylon.

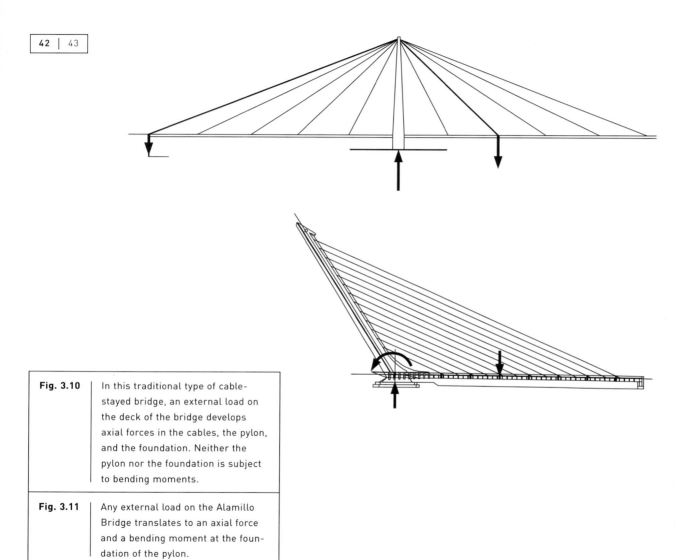

The external loads of any structure are transferred to the foundation. Equilibrium under changing loading conditions is reached by developing the needed reaction forces at the supports (fig. 3.10). The Alamillo Bridge relies on a single support at the foundation of the pylon to withstand any loading changes.

Varying loading conditions resulting from live, thermal, wind, and seismic loads are expected to change the magnitude of the axial forces of the cable stays, thus creating eccentricities that cause bending moments at the foundation of the pylon in all directions. Furthermore, transverse loading of the pylon will cause bending moments in the other direction—in the same direction as the torsional moment that the steel box carries to the foundation. The pylon foundation, then, should constrain all six degrees of freedom, countering reaction forces and moments that are expected to be quite large (fig. 3.11). Furthermore, a strong vertical support is needed for the weight of the pylon and the vertical loads along the steel box, transferred through the cable stays to the pylon.

The east abutment is expected to experience significantly smaller reactions than the foundation

| **Fig. 3.10** | In this traditional type of cable-stayed bridge, an external load on the deck of the bridge develops axial forces in the cables, the pylon, and the foundation. Neither the pylon nor the foundation is subject to bending moments. |
| **Fig. 3.11** | Any external load on the Alamillo Bridge translates to an axial force and a bending moment at the foundation of the pylon. |

of the pylon. The east abutment should provide a minimal vertical support at the end of the box, withstanding the loads on the last portion of the deck that is not supported by the cable stays, and should support the steel box for the torsion resulting from unbalanced live load on the deck. It should also constrain the horizontal movement perpendicular to the axis of the deck to withstand environmental loads, while it should not constrain the expansion of the deck along its longitudinal axis, or rotations of the longitudinal axis of the bridge (fig. 3.12).

Fig. 3.12 | The constrained degrees of freedom in the east abutment, on the Seville side, are: transverse displacement (z), upward displacement (y), and rotation along the longitudinal axis of the bridge (torsion).

Fig. 3.13 | The bridge without the cables and without the east abutment, subject to the dead weight of the deck and the pylon. The bending moments (in MN-m) of the freestanding members and their deflection are shown for comparison.

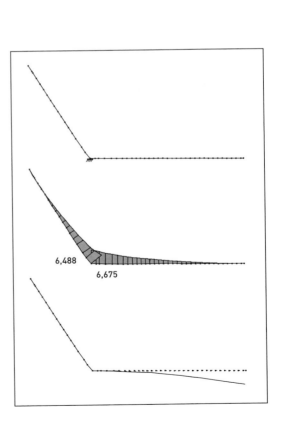

3.2
A STATICALLY
INDETERMINATE STRUCTURE

The Alamillo Bridge has been designed as a statically indeterminate structure. Without the thirteen pairs of cable stays and the east abutment, the bridge reduces to a statically determinate structure composed of two cantilevers (fig. 3.13). Although such a structure could not have the necessary strength to carry the loads along a 200 m span, it is shown here to illustrate a statically determinate structure, in which the bending moments of both the pylon and the deck are subject to their own dead weight, without cables, supported by a mo-

ment-resisting foundation. The actual geometry and weight of the pylon and the deck, as they have been constructed, are used in these calculations. As a simple cantilever, the equilibrium of the pylon would depend on its fixed support on the ground. The calculated bending moment at the base of the pylon would reach 6,500 million newton-meters (MN-m), and the calculated deflection at its top would exceed 3.2 m. These magnitudes suggest that the inclined pylon could not support itself and needs the support provided by the cables. The bending moment at the base of the pylon is very close to the bending moment at the beginning of

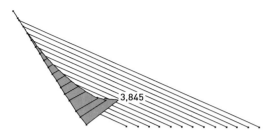

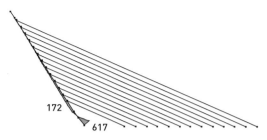

the deck, indicating a near balance under dead weights. Under those conditions, the foundation takes almost no moment and a vertical reaction of 266 MN. The deflection of the two cantilevers (fig. 3.13) demonstrates the stiffness of the pylon as compared to that of the deck.

Any structure deforms under loading, and its structural elements are subject to deformations corresponding to the internal forces in each member. For a statically indeterminate structure, the deformations of the structural elements at equilibrium (and hence the distribution of forces among them) depend on the relative stiffness of those elements. Thus the deck and the pylon of the Alamillo Bridge are deformed and stressed as the cable stays reach the required deformation for equilibrium. As a consequence of the statically indeterminate structure, the relative stiffness of the pylon, the

deck, and the cables, as well as the magnitude of the post-tension of the cables, are vital variables in the relative deformation of those elements and the distribution of forces.

In the model shown in fig. 3.14, the pylon is supported by the cables while its connection to the foundation is rigid. The pylon has reached equilibrium, relying partially on the cables and partially on its own fixed foundation. The actual sizes of the cables and the pylon have been used for this model. The cables are connected to the pylon by pin connections; at the opposite end, where they should be connected to the deck, they are supported on hinges. Such a boundary condition implies that the deck is infinitely stiff, an assumption that is satisfactory for the scope of this model. Compared to the model of the freestanding pylon, the addition of the cables reduces the bending moments along

| Fig. 3.14 | The equilibrium of the pylon when supported by cables without post-tension (left) and when the cables are post-tensioned (right). Bending moments in MN-m. |

the pylon. However, the cables are relatively soft compared to the stiffness of the pylon, and they are not stressed adequately (table 3.1). Thus, significant bending moments still develop (fig. 3.14, left); the bending moment at the foundation is 3,845 MN-m, a 41% reduction of the bending moment developed without the cables. In order to increase the effectiveness of the cables, they must be post-tensioned to reach a desired level of force before the pylon experiences any deformations (fig. 3.14, right).

Table 3.1 The forces and the stresses in each pair of cables that develop from supporting the fixed pylon, without post-tension.

Pair of cables	Force (MN)	Stress (kPa)
1	2.80	16.3
2	3.50	20.3
3	4.16	24.2
4	4.76	27.7
5	5.27	30.6
6	5.72	33.3
7	6.13	35.6
8	6.49	37.8
9	6.81	39.6
10	7.09	41.3
11	7.35	42.7
12	7.57	44.0
13	5.83	46.3

The constraints from the cables that make the bridge statically indeterminate are internal to the structure, so the bridge can be displaced as a rigid body without developing additional stresses as a result of that movement. The only external constraints on a rigid body movement of the bridge come from the foundation of the pylon (six constrained degrees of freedom) and the east abutment (three constrained degrees of freedom). Thus, the bridge has three additional degrees of freedom constrained beyond those of a statically determinate structure. The structural elements of the bridge have been designed to have sufficient strength to accommodate certain settlements and rotation of the supports.

3.3
CHOICE OF MATERIALS AND DIMENSIONS

The materials of the structural elements and their dimensions are required as input for a finite element analysis to determine the forces in the various structural elements of the statically indeterminate bridge. So, although the final selection of materials is made according to an iterative process, based on the results of the finite element analysis itself, certain assumptions had to be made before the execution of the computer-based analysis. Most of these were dictated by the design intentions both for the general shape of the bridge and for its details.

The preliminary design was based on the anticipated live loads and a rough estimate of the dead loads of the structural elements that are required to support those live loads. According to Spanish code,[3] the live load for bridges built for vehicular traffic should be a uniform load of 4 kilopascals (kPa) acting on the surface of the deck as well as on the pedestrian walkways, plus a simultaneous load from a single truck weighing 600 kilonewtons (kN) on each side of the roadway. The load of the truck should be distributed as six loads of 100 kN (fig. 3.15); the surface area of each of these is approximated as a rectangle measuring 0.20 m by 0.60 m, indicating the footprint of a truck's wheel, with the longer dimension running along the transverse axis of the road. Since live loads may not be present on the bridge, the equilibrium of the bridge must be calculated both with and without the live loads.

3 Instrucción Relativa a las Acciones a considerar en el Proyecto de Puentes de Carreteras, MOPT, 28 February 1972.

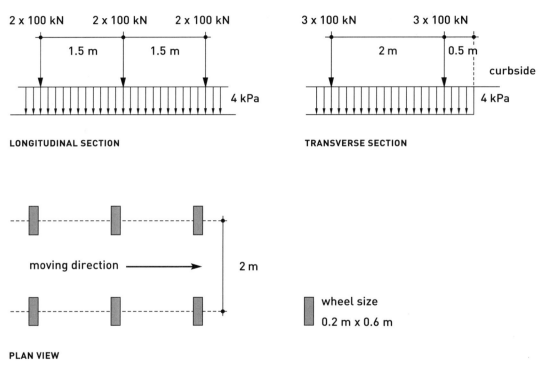

2 x 100 kN   **2 x 100 kN**   **2 x 100 kN**

1.5 m   1.5 m

4 kPa

LONGITUDINAL SECTION

3 x 100 kN   **3 x 100 kN**

2 m   0.5 m

curbside

4 kPa

TRANSVERSE SECTION

moving direction ——————→   2 m

PLAN VIEW

■ wheel size
■ 0.2 m x 0.6 m

| **Fig. 3.15** | The live loads acting on a bridge for vehicular traffic, according to Spanish regulations. |

3.3.1
THE PRELIMINARY DESIGN
OF THE DECK

For the general equilibrium, the weight of the deck should be as light as possible, so that its load on the cable stays and the pylon is minimal. Initially, the deck of the Alamillo Bridge was conceived to be constructed in concrete, counting on the long Spanish tradition of generating artful forms and craftsmanship in concrete construction. However, the tripartite articulation of the deck—the center box and the two roadways—did not provide a strong argument for using concrete (which would have been more appropriate had the overall section of the deck formed a single large box). Furthermore, as opposed to concrete, steel construction for the deck would reduce the deck's dead weight and could be built in a shorter time. The prefabricated modular steel elements of the box and the wings would be faster to assemble in situ than would prefabricated concrete elements.

Once it was decided that the box and the cantilevers would be made of steel, the weight of the deck could be determined. The concrete slabs forming the roadways were designed to support the live load as defined by the applicable code requirements. The steel cantilevers were designed to support the concrete slab and its live load. As the cables were to support the deck every 12 m, the grid for the cantilevers was set to 4 m, or three pairs of cantilevers for every pair of cables.

The steel box was designed primarily for bending and torsion. With respect to bending, the box is a continuous beam supported by the two abutments and the cable stays. To determine the bending moments in the box, one needs to know the relative stiffness of the cable stays as compared to the box's own stiffness; a first approximation could assume that the dead and permanent loads stress the steel box only minimally after the cables are post-tensioned. The steel box then behaves as a fixed-hinged beam, subject to the live load. The uniform live load acting on the entire surface of the deck yields a uniform load per length:

$$w_l = 4 \text{ kPa} \times 32 \text{ m} = 128 \text{ kN/m} \qquad (3.1)$$

Taking into account the relatively stiff end of the deck at the base of the pylon, where part of the box is filled with concrete, one can assume an effective length of the steel box equal to 140 m. Such an assumption suggests a maximum bending moment for a fixed-pinned beam:

$$M = \frac{w_l \times (0.75 L_{eff})^2}{8}$$
$$= \frac{0.128 \times (0.75 \times 140)^2}{8}$$
$$\rightarrow M = 176.4 \text{ MN-m} \qquad (3.2)$$

The bending moment diagram shown in fig. 3.16 is based on the above data and assumptions and could be used for the preliminary dimensioning of the box.

The maximum torsional load on the 170 m long steel box occurs when the deck on one side of the steel box is completely loaded and the other side of the deck is empty. Thus, the uniform live load of 4 kPa develops a uniform torque per unit length equal to 4 kPa $\times$ 16 m $\times$ 8 m = 510 kN-m/m. In addition, the 600 kN truck develops a torque of 8 MN-m. In order to carry the torsional loads, the steel box is supported on both sides so that it cannot twist. The maximum torque T_{max} occurs at each support, calculated to be:

$$T_{max} = \frac{1}{2} \times 0.51 \times (170 + 8)$$
$$= 47.4 \text{ MN-m} \qquad (3.3)$$

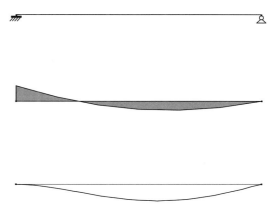

Fig. 3.16 | A first approximation of the bending moments and the deflections of the steel box.

The steel box is designed to withstand that torque as a thin-wall hollow section, developing a maximum shearing stress τ_{max} due to torsion:

$$\tau_{max} = \frac{T_{max}}{2 \times t \times A} = \frac{47.4}{2 \times 0.05 \times 20}$$
$$= 23.7 \text{ MPa} \qquad (3.4)$$

where T_{max} is the torque at the specific cross section, t is the wall thickness of the hollow section, equal to 50 mm, and A is the area of the hollow section bounded by the centerline of the thin wall, equal to 20 m² (shown in fig. 3.17 as gray area).

3.3.2
THE POST-TENSIONING OF THE CABLE STAYS

After the deck was given its preliminary design, that of the pylon and the cable stays followed. Fig. 3.18 shows the equilibrium of the forces in the bridge at three nodes: the connection of a pair of cables with the pylon, the connection of a pair of cables with the deck, and the foundation of the pylon.

The equilibrium at the pylon under funicular loading, based on the 58° slope of the pylon and the 24° slope of the cables, reveals that the post-tension force (T) in each pair of cables should be almost equal in magnitude to the weight of the corresponding segment of the pylon (W_P) that the pair of cables supports:

$$T = W_P \qquad (3.5)$$

The weight of the segment of the deck (W_D) supported by that pair of cables, for funicular loading, is calculated to be:

$$W_D = T\sin24° = W_P\sin24° \qquad (3.6)$$

Furthermore, the horizontal component of the force along the deck (F_D) should be:

$$F_D = T\cos24° = \frac{W_D}{\tan24°} = 2.25\,W_D \qquad (3.7)$$

F_D is equal and opposite to the corresponding horizontal component of the force at the base of the pylon, setting the deck in compression and relieving the foundation from a horizontal force.

As the weight of the pylon changes along its length because of the changing geometry of the cross section, the post-tensioning forces should vary from cable to cable under the funicular loading condition. Table 3.2 presents the actual post-tensioning force for each pair of cables and the weight of each segment of the pylon, as constructed. According to the table, the longest cable has the least force, while the shortest cable has the greatest force. Furthermore, since the cables cannot have the same post-tension force, the funicular loading condition requires a deck with variable dead weight along its length. Placing concrete inside the steel box of the deck close to the pylon assisted in securing those different weights along the deck. The last two columns of table 3.2 show the estimated weight for each segment of the deck, according to expression (3.6), and the actual weight of that segment as constructed.

For the calculated loads, the cables were assembled using 60 strands of steel measuring 15.2 mm in diameter each, yielding a cross-sectional area of 8,450 mm² and a weight of 755 N/m, except for the cables of the longest pair which were made of 45 strands, yielding an area of 6,340 mm² and a weight of 583 N/m. Subject to their own weight, the cables take the form of the catenary (fig. 3.19), sagging in the middle and providing a smaller effective area than the actual area of their cross section to withstand the externally applied loads. Table 3.3 presents the tension force in each cable, its length, total weight and sag, and its effective area to be used as input in the finite ele-

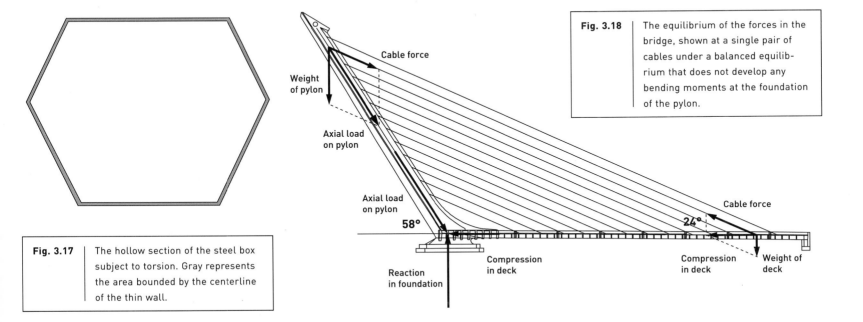

Fig. 3.18 | The equilibrium of the forces in the bridge, shown at a single pair of cables under a balanced equilibrium that does not develop any bending moments at the foundation of the pylon.

Cable force

Weight of pylon

Axial load on pylon

Axial load on pylon

58°

Reaction in foundation

Compression in deck

Cable force

24°

Compression in deck

Weight of deck

Fig. 3.17 | The hollow section of the steel box subject to torsion. Gray represents the area bounded by the centerline of the thin wall.

Table 3.2 The weight of each caisson of the pylon, including the enclosed concrete, the post-tension of the cables, and the ideal weight of the deck.

Caisson no.	Cable no.	Weight of caisson, actual (MN)	Post-tension of cables, actual (MN)	Weight of deck, estimated (MN)	Weight of deck, actual (MN)
4	1 (shortest)	14.39	10.97	4.46	5.68
5	2	11.62	11.26	4.58	5.68
6	3	11.04	11.56	4.70	4.12
7	4	10.57	9.63	3.91	4.12
8	5	9.83	9.83	4.00	3.83
9	6	10.24	10.05	4.08	3.83
10	7	11.04	10.20	4.15	3.84
11	8	10.43	10.08	4.10	3.84
12	9	9.77	9.93	4.04	3.97
13	10	9.38	9.85	4.00	3.97
14	11	8.90	9.67	3.93	3.93
15	12	8.47	9.59	3.90	3.93
16 + head	13 (longest)	9.01	9.50	3.87	3.60

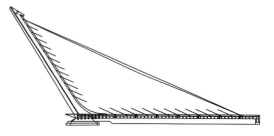

Fig. 3.19 The cables take the shape of the catenary as a result of their own weight. The anchorages should be designed for the end angles, as calculated in table 3.3, to avoid bending moments.

ment program. The data in table 3.3 derive from the coordinates of the end points of each cable, the cable's weight, the post-tensioning force, and the modulus of elasticity $E = 200,000$ MPa. The longer cables are quite heavy and they experience a significant deflection, reaching a sag equal to 1/170 of the length for the cables of the 12th pair. The cables in the 13th pair were designed to be smaller in di-

ameter and therefore lighter, in order to avoid even more sagging. This was feasible because this pair connects to the lighter upper part of the pylon and to the part of the deck nearest to the east abutment.

The cables of the 13th pair are quite long. If they were the longest cables of a conventional cable-stayed bridge, with the same 24° inclination with the horizontal, they could sustain two 280 m

Table 3.3 Data for each deformed cable, subject to its own weight and the post-tension force.

Cable	Horizontal force (MN)	Length (m)	Cable weight (kN)	Angle at deck	Angle at pylon	Sag (m)	Effective area (mm²)	Area loss	Length/sag
1	5.30	75.875	57.29	24.252	24.764	0.093	8,435	0%	816
2	5.43	94.234	71.22	24.180	24.801	0.140	8,428	0%	673
3	5.58	112.497	84.95	24.123	24.846	0.195	8,421	0%	577
4	4.74	130.426	98.52	23.990	24.976	0.308	8,387	1%	423
5	4.83	148.339	112.05	23.938	25.038	0.391	8,374	1%	379
6	4.63	166.266	125.59	23.849	25.136	0.513	8,341	1%	324
7	4.67	184.217	139.15	23.786	25.201	0.625	8,320	2%	295
8	4.63	202.141	152.69	23.715	25.281	0.759	8,290	2%	266
9	4.53	220.072	166.28	23.631	25.372	0.919	8,249	2%	239
10	4.26	238.008	179.79	23.501	25.505	1.144	8,170	3%	208
11	4.11	255.209	193.33	23.390	25.623	1.371	8,092	4%	186
12	4.00	273.882	206.88	23.284	25.736	1.611	8,012	5%	170
13	4.29	291.834	170.20	23.575	25.457	1.317	6,200	2%	222

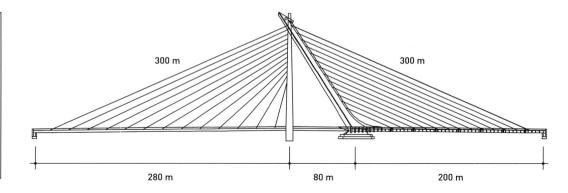

300 m   300 m

280 m   80 m   200 m

long clear spans of a deck on each side of the pylon, assuming a similar deck weight and similar live loads (fig. 3.20).

3.3.3
THE PRELIMINARY DESIGN
OF THE PYLON

For equilibrium, the pylon was designed to be heavy, and considerations of weight governed its preliminary design. Calculations on the geometry of the bridge for the funicular loading condition reveal that the weight of the pylon per unit length (w_P) should be 3.4 times the weight of the deck per unit length (w_D):

$$L_{P_y} = L_P \sin 58°$$
$$= (L_D + L_P \cos 58°)\tan 24° \qquad (3.8)$$

$$L_P = L_D \frac{\tan 24°}{\sin 58° - \cos 58° \tan 24°}$$
$$= 8.73 \text{ m} \qquad (3.9)$$

$$L_{P_y} = L_P \sin 58° = 7.40 \text{ m} \qquad (3.10)$$

$$W_D = T\sin 24° = W_P \sin 24° \qquad (3.11)$$

$$w_D \times L_D = w_P \times L_P \sin 24° \qquad (3.12)$$

$$\frac{w_P}{w_D} = \frac{L_D}{L_P \sin 24°} \rightarrow$$

$$\frac{w_P}{w_D} = \frac{\sin 58° - \cos 58° \tan 24°}{\tan 24° \sin 24°} = 3.4 \qquad (3.13)$$

where L_D is the length of the segment of the deck that corresponds to a pair of cables, L_P is the length of the segment of the pylon that corresponds to a pair of cables, and L_{P_y} is the vertical projection of L_P.

A concrete pylon could provide the necessary weight. The design requirement for a changing cross section of the pylon along its length, as well as details of the steel reinforcement, led to a composite design of steel caissons forming the outer surface of the pylon and reinforced concrete filling them. Table 3.2 presents the total weight of each segment of the pylon as constructed.

4 STRUCTURAL ANALYSIS AND DESIGN

Live, thermal, wind, and seismic loads, along with foundation settlements, make the equilibrium of the Alamillo Bridge more complex in terms of identifying which load combination should correspond to the funicular loading. Thus, a comprehensible finite element model was employed to analyze the bridge under the applicable loading conditions and to perform feasibility studies. Angel Aparicio, Professor of Structures at the School of Civil Engineering of the Technical University of Barcelona,[1] used the model to provide the necessary information for the dimensioning of the bridge's structural elements and to determine the loads on the foundation.[2]

Finite element analysis provides the forces and stresses, as well as the deformations of a structure subject to certain loading conditions. The input for a finite element analysis consists of the geometry of the structure, the mechanical properties of the materials, a description of the structural supports, and the applied loads. The structure is treated as a finite number of discrete elements. The elements in the analysis can be linear, planar, or solid, and each element approximates the behavior of a corresponding segment of the physical structure.[3] The elements are connected at nodes. The nodes have no physical properties other than that they provide the coordinates for joining the elements together. The nodes represent rigid connections unless some free degrees of freedom are allowed. A series of loads are applied on the nodes or on the elements themselves.

Following the input of the geometry of the structure, the materials of the elements, and the externally applied loads, a computer program assembles a series of linear "stiffness" equations. The unknowns in these equations are the displacements and rotations of the degrees of freedom of the structure, so the number of unknowns for a three-dimensional structure is equal to six times the number of nodes. The number of equations is equal to the number of unknowns, so the computer can solve the linear system of equations—which can easily reach the thousands. The solution gives the displacements and rotations of each node. Then, each element is subject to the displacements and rotations of its own nodes to determine the internal forces and the stresses of the element.

For linear analysis, the stresses are always proportional to the strains, regardless of their magnitude. Nonlinear analysis is meaningful when the constitutive law of the material is nonlinear (material nonlinearity), or when the geometry of the structure may buckle (geometric nonlinearity), like the pylon in the Alamillo Bridge. Nonlinear analysis requires a series of solutions to the simultaneous equations, applying the external loads at small increments on the deformed structure and obtaining the further deformations in small increments as well.

In finite element analysis, the properties of the elements are required as input, yet the output determines their structural sufficiency. As discussed in chapter 3, the Alamillo Bridge is statically indeterminate, and any significant changes in the stiffness of its elements (i.e., changes in their cross-sectional shape) would cause a redistribution of forces among the elements of the bridge. Thus, an iterative design process was followed. During this process, the output of a finite element analysis served to redesign the elements of the bridge, and a new analysis was based on the updated properties of the elements.

4.1
THE FINITE ELEMENT MODEL

The finite element model that was used for the analysis of the bridge is shown in fig. 4.1 superimposed on the elevation of the bridge. It includes elements for the steel box, the cable stays, and the pylon only. The slab of the roadways and the cantilevering girders are not included in the model since they act independently for most loading cases and do not add stiffness or strength to the deck. The model consists of 51 nodes, 50 beam elements, and 13 cable elements. Although all the elements are on a single plane, the model is three-dimensional, having six degrees of freedom on each node: three displacements and three rota-

1 Catedrático de Estructuras de la Escuela Técnica Superior de Ingenieros de Caminos, Canales y Puertos de la Universidad Politécnica de Barcelona.

2 For the purposes of this book, Multiframe-3D of Formation Design Systems (www.formsys.com) was used to duplicate the structural analysis of the bridge, to perform feasibility studies, and to produce the graphic displays.

3 Some elements, such as beams, trusses, or cables, simulate accurately the corresponding physical segment of the structure. These elements have been used in the model of the Alamillo Bridge.

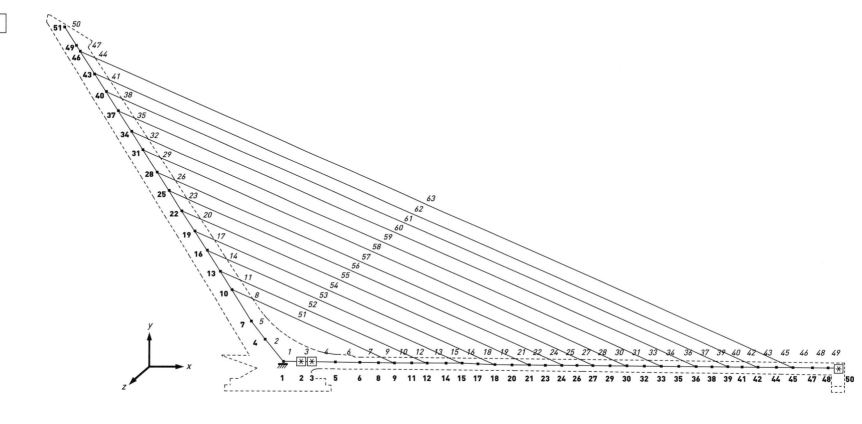

Fig. 4.1 | The finite element model of the Alamillo Bridge, superimposed on the bridge's elevation.

Bold numbers indicate nodes; see table 4.1

Italic numbers indicate elements; see table 4.4

⊞ Special support; see table 4.2

▨ Fixed support

Table 4.1 The coordinates of the nodes for the finite element model, in meters.

Node	x	y	z	Node	x	y	z
1	1.00	13.50	0.00	27	113.60	12.12	0.00
2	7.61	13.30	0.00	28	−44.95	84.33	0.00
3	11.65	13.18	0.00	29	119.57	12.06	0.00
4	−5.58	21.57	0.00	30	125.54	12.00	0.00
5	19.72	12.94	0.00	31	−49.47	91.73	0.00
6	28.43	12.68	0.00	32	131.53	11.93	0.00
7	−10.28	28.29	0.00	33	137.52	11.87	0.00
8	35.64	12.50	0.00	34	−54.00	99.12	0.00
9	42.85	12.32	0.00	35	143.49	11.80	0.00
10	−17.55	39.82	0.00	36	149.45	11.74	0.00
11	48.99	12.20	0.00	37	−58.52	106.52	0.00
12	55.15	12.09	0.00	38	155.41	11.68	0.00
13	−22.10	47.23	0.00	39	161.37	11.62	0.00
14	60.86	12.15	0.00	40	−63.04	113.92	0.00
15	66.58	12.22	0.00	41	167.33	11.56	0.00
16	−26.65	54.65	0.00	42	173.30	11.49	0.00
17	72.21	12.33	0.00	43	−67.56	121.32	0.00
18	77.83	12.43	0.00	44	179.30	11.43	0.00
19	−31.19	62.04	0.00	45	185.31	11.36	0.00
20	83.79	12.38	0.00	46	−72.10	128.76	0.00
21	89.75	12.33	0.00	47	191.70	11.29	0.00
22	−35.75	69.46	0.00	48	197.70	11.23	0.00
23	95.71	12.28	0.00	49	−73.43	130.94	0.00
24	101.67	12.22	0.00	50	201.00	11.20	0.00
25	−40.34	76.89	0.00	51	−78.21	138.75	0.00
26	107.64	12.17	0.00				

tions. The geometry of the model, updated to incorporate the final geometry of the bridge as built, provides the coordinates of the nodes (table 4.1) and shows the constrained degrees of freedom of the finite element model that correspond to the support conditions (table 4.2). The structural materials consist of steel for the box and the caissons of the pylon, reinforced concrete for the pylon and the part of the deck near the pedestal of the pylon, and high-strength steel for the cable stays. An analysis of the mechanical properties of the pylon and the deck shows equivalent properties of concrete sections. These values have been obtained by transforming the sections of steel in both the pylon and the deck to equivalent concrete sections. Thus, the analysis of each element is based on a single material.

Table 4.3 shows the mechanical properties of the structural materials of the Alamillo Bridge. Table 4.4 illustrates the connectivity arrays among elements and nodes, as well as the mechanical properties of the cross sections of the elements. The finite element model was subjected to 25 independent loading conditions (table 4.5). The results of these loading conditions were combined to produce the specific loading conditions incorporated into the design of the bridge.

Table 4.2 The constrained degrees of freedom of the finite element model.

Node	x-displacement	y-displacement	z-displacement	x-rotation	y-rotation	z-rotation
1	Fixed	Fixed	Fixed	Fixed	Fixed	Fixed
2	Free	Fixed	Fixed	Fixed	Free	Free
3	Free	Fixed	Fixed	Fixed	Free	Free
50	Free	Fixed	Fixed	Fixed	Free	Free

Table 4.3 The materials used for the analysis and the construction of the bridge.

Structural steel	Plates	A52d
	IPE 600	A52d
	HEB 600	A52d
	L 120×120×12 (mm)	A42b
Reinforced concrete	Leveling/ground slabs	H-100 (compression strength: 10 MPa)
	Piles of foundation	H-200 (compression strength: 20 MPa)
	Pedestal	H-300 (compression strength: 30 MPa)
	Superstructure	H-350 (compression strength: 35 MPa)
	Reinforcing steel	Corrugated AEH-500 (yield strength: 500 MPa)

For an ultimate strength design, according to the Spanish code for reinforced concrete, the strength of the materials must be reduced by 0.90 for the reinforcing steel and 0.67 for the concrete, and the dead and live loads must be amplified by 1.5.

Table 4.4 The connectivity arrays of the members for the finite element model and their cross-sectional properties. The cables are made of steel ($E = 200,000$ MPa), while the sectional properties for both the pylon and the deck are given in equivalent concrete sections ($E = 29,430$ MPa).

	Member	Start node	End node	Area (m²)	Moment of inertia z (m⁴)	Moment of inertia y (m⁴)	Modulus of torsion (m⁴)
Pylon	2	1	4	86.0600	1048.40	524.44	721.30
	5	4	7	68.3300	625.90	423.43	424.70
	8	7	10	62.9000	512.70	374.38	321.83
	11	10	13	56.8000	428.90	354.31	293.87
	14	13	16	54.1500	393.20	334.82	267.32
	17	16	19	51.7100	361.73	315.92	242.20
	20	19	22	48.9500	327.90	297.58	218.45
	23	22	25	46.5700	300.05	279.78	196.11
	26	25	28	53.2900	278.64	268.43	175.12
	29	28	31	50.9600	253.40	257.61	155.49
	32	31	34	48.6500	229.90	241.41	137.19
	35	34	37	46.0400	205.01	225.72	120.20
	38	37	40	43.7800	184.90	210.54	104.51
	41	40	43	41.2300	163.75	195.85	90.07
	44	43	46	39.0200	146.72	181.63	76.89
	47	46	49	37.4600	135.37	167.89	64.91
	50	49	51	37.4600	135.37	167.89	64.91
Cables	51	9	10	0.0016870	0.00	0.00	0.00
	52	12	13	0.0016856	0.00	0.00	0.00
	53	15	16	0.0016842	0.00	0.00	0.00
	54	18	19	0.0016774	0.00	0.00	0.00
	55	21	22	0.0016748	0.00	0.00	0.00
	56	24	25	0.0016682	0.00	0.00	0.00
	57	27	28	0.0016640	0.00	0.00	0.00
	58	30	31	0.0016580	0.00	0.00	0.00
	59	33	34	0.0016498	0.00	0.00	0.00

Table 4.4 cont'd

	Member	Start node	End node	Area (m²)	Moment of inertia z (m⁴)	Moment of inertia y (m⁴)	Modulus of torsion (m⁴)
Cables (cont'd)	60	36	37	0.0016340	0.00	0.00	0.00
	61	39	40	0.0016184	0.00	0.00	0.00
	62	42	43	0.0016024	0.00	0.00	0.00
	63	45	46	0.0012400	0.00	0.00	0.00
Deck	1	1	2	82.2400	672.00	946.30	92.90
	3	2	3	60.9900	327.80	724.50	92.90
	4	3	5	40.3000	95.92	572.90	92.90
	6	5	6	33.2900	61.03	449.80	89.93
	7	6	8	33.3700	68.44	371.83	69.83
	9	8	9	26.2200	61.60	304.29	49.74
	10	9	11	17.0200	41.47	248.56	39.64
	12	11	12	14.2200	33.91	233.18	34.90
	13	12	14	12.8400	31.61	232.17	32.50
	15	14	15	11.7000	29.69	220.82	31.60
	16	15	17	10.7000	26.91	219.00	31.60
	18	17	18	9.4600	21.67	217.51	31.60
	19	18	20	9.4600	21.67	217.51	31.60
	21	20	21	9.1300	21.12	216.04	28.80

	Member	Start node	End node	Area (m²)	Moment of inertia z (m⁴)	Moment of inertia y (m⁴)	Modulus of torsion (m⁴)
Deck (cont'd)	22	21	23	8.7900	20.57	214.57	26.10
	24	23	24	8.7900	20.57	214.57	26.10
	25	24	26	8.9300	21.04	214.70	26.50
	27	26	27	8.9300	21.04	214.70	26.50
	28	27	29	8.9300	21.04	214.70	26.50
	30	29	30	8.9300	21.04	214.70	26.50
	31	30	32	8.9300	21.04	214.70	26.50
	33	32	33	9.2600	21.63	216.17	29.30
	34	33	35	9.6000	22.15	217.64	32.20
	36	35	36	9.6000	22.15	217.64	32.20
	37	36	38	9.6000	22.15	217.64	32.20
	39	38	39	9.6000	22.15	217.64	32.20
	40	39	41	9.6000	22.15	217.64	32.20
	42	41	42	9.6000	22.15	217.64	32.20
	43	42	44	9.4600	21.67	217.51	31.60
	45	44	45	9.4600	21.67	217.51	31.60
	46	45	47	9.4600	21.67	217.51	31.60
	48	47	48	9.4600	21.67	217.51	31.60
	49	48	50	9.4600	21.67	217.51	31.60

Table 4.5 The 25 independent load combinations that were considered for the analysis and design of the Alami-llo Bridge.

1. Dead and permanent loads	1.1	Dead and permanent loads of the pylon, W_{pylon}
	1.2	Dead and permanent loads of the deck, W_{deck}
	1.3	Post-tension of the cable stays, T_{cables}
2. Live loads	2.1	Uniform load 4 KPa on the entire deck and the pedestrian walkway
	2.2	Uniform load 4 KPa on half the deck and half the pedestrian walkway (to produce maximum torsion on the steel box)
	2.3	600 kN truck load at node 6 (axis 44; 172 m from the east abutment), eccentricity 13.30 m
	2.4	600 kN truck load at node 9 (axis 41; 160 m from the east abutment), eccentricity 13.30 m
	2.5	600 kN truck load at node 15 (axis 35; 136 m from the east abutment), eccentricity 13.30 m
	2.6	600 kN truck load at node 21 (axis 29; 104 m from the east abutment), eccentricity 13.30 m
	2.7	600 kN truck load at node 27 (axis 23; 88 m from the east abutment), eccentricity 13.30 m
	2.8	600 kN truck load at node 33 (axis 17; 64 m from the east abutment), eccentricity 13.30 m
	2.9	600 kN truck load at node 39 (axis 11; 40 m from the east abutment), eccentricity 13.30 m
	2.10	600 kN truck load at node 45 (axis 5; 16 m from the east abutment), eccentricity 13.30 m
3. Thermal loads	3.1	Uniform change in temperature of the cables by 26°C
	3.2	Uniform change in temperature of the pylon by 13.5°C
	3.3	Uniform change in temperature of the deck by 23.3°C
	3.4	Linear variation of temperature within the deck (lower to upper surface) by 21°C
	3.5	Linear longitudinal variation of temperature within the pylon by 4.5°C
	3.6	Linear transverse variation of temperature within the pylon by 5.1°C
4. Static wind loads	4.1	Longitudinal wind load
	4.2	Transverse wind load
5. Rotation of the foundation of the pylon	5.1	0.25% (0.225°) rotation in the longitudinal direction; maximum predicted rotation 0.06°
	5.2	0.10% (0.090°) rotation in the transverse direction; maximum predicted rotation 0.026°
6. Static seismic loads	6.1	Longitudinal seismic load on the pylon (3% of dead load)
	6.2	Transverse seismic load on the pylon (3% of dead load)

	Member	Distributed load (kN/m)	Segment (if not uniform)			Member	Distributed load (kN/m)
pylon	2	3,360			deck	4	1,169
	5	2,920				6	900
	8	2,766				7	800
	11	2,698				9	658
	14	2,578				10	463
	17	2,457				12	432
	20	2,336				13	405
	23	2,212				15	382
	26	2,499	0.00–0.91			16	313
		2,119	0.91–1.00			18	313
	29	2,441				19	313
	32	2,322				21	305
	35	2,215				22	305
	38	2,104				24	305
	41	1,995				25	305
	44	1,887				27	306
	47	1,673	0.00–0.47			28	306
		1,765	0.47–0.79			30	306
		1,807	0.79–1.00			31	306
	50	2,003	0.69–1.00			33	306
						34	306
						36	306
						37	306
						40	306
						42	306
						39	307
						43	305
						46	305
						45	304
						48	304
						49	304

Table 4.6 The distributed dead load on the finite elements of the pylon and the deck. For the elements of the pylon, the distributed load is given per projected unit length on the horizontal axis.

4.2
DEAD AND PERMANENT LOADS

The dead loads originate from the weight of the bridge's structural elements. Table 4.6 shows the dead load of each finite element of the pylon and the deck. For the finite elements of the pylon, the

Table 4.7 The post-tensioning force for each pair of cables.

Pair of cables	Post-tension force (kN)
1 (shortest)	10,968
2	11,262
3	11,556
4	9,633
5	9,830
6	10,045
7	10,202
8	10,085
9	9,928
10	9,849
11	9,673
12	9,594
13 (longest)	9,496

load is distributed per projected length along the horizontal axis. According to the data in this table, the total weight of the pylon above the pedestal is 185 MN, and the total weight of the deck is 81 MN, corresponding to a ratio of 2.3:1. The bridge has a total deck surface of 232 m $\times$ 32 m = 7,424 m²; thus the 266 MN dead weight of the superstructure corresponds to a uniform load of 36 kPa, distributed on the entire surface of the bridge. The dead load of the bridge amounts to almost 9 times the live load, which is almost 4.1 kPa, including the 600 kN truck load.

The permanent loads consist of the weight of nonstructural elements, or loads on structural elements that are an inherent part of the bridge but may be removed temporarily in the future. The post-tensioning forces in the cable stays are the predominant permanent loads on the Alamillo Bridge. Their magnitude (table 4.7) is comparable to the dead weight of the deck and the pylon. Pavement, railings, lighting fixtures, etc., are additional permanent loads. Compared to the magnitude of the dead loads, those loads are very small and no further distinction need be made between the dead loads and those permanent loads.

A major concern with the dead and permanent loads of the bridge came from the sensitivity of the equilibrium of the bridge to changing loads. Even small deviations in the weight of the elements during construction could cause unbalanced forces and undue stresses. As its equilibrium depends on the relative weight of its structural elements and a single moment-resisting foundation, a quite unusual analysis was required. A sensitivity analysis of the dead and permanent loads was performed to study the effect of deviations on the bending moments at critical sections of the bridge. In that analysis, the dead loads were handled separately for the pylon and the deck. Then, the following five load variations were considered, reflecting tolerances in construction:

$$W_{deck} + W_{pylon} + T_{cables} \qquad (4.1)$$

$$W_{deck} + W_{pylon} + 0.9 \times T_{cables} \qquad (4.2)$$

$$W_{deck} + W_{pylon} + 1.1 \times T_{cables} \qquad (4.3)$$

$$0.9 \times W_{deck} + 1.1 \times W_{pylon} + T_{cables} \qquad (4.4)$$

$$1.1 \times W_{deck} + 0.9 \times W_{pylon} + T_{cables} \qquad (4.5)$$

The bending moment diagrams for the above five load variations are presented in fig. 4.2, together with the corresponding deflection diagrams.

The bending moments at four critical sections of the bridge (fig. 4.3) provide a measure of the variation in the bending moments from those five combinations of loads. Table 4.8 summarizes the obtained results.

Foundation of the pylon. Under loading condition (4.5), the bending moment increases 120% over the bending moment for loading condition (4.1), which constitutes the basic hypothesis. Furthermore, there is a reversal of bending moments under conditions (4.3) and (4.4): while the bending moments under loading conditions (4.1), (4.2), and (4.5) correspond to compression in the lower side of the pylon, the bending moments under loading conditions (4.3) and (4.4) correspond to tension in that area.

Axis 47: transition from the steel box to the concrete section of the deck. There is no reversal of the bending moments in that section where the lower fibers of the deck are in tension. However, there is a major variation in bending moments, from 0 to −506 MN-m, the latter corresponding to loading condition (4.4).

Axis 41: deck section at the anchorage of cable stays no. 1. There is no reversal of bending mo-ments for this section either. However, there is a 100% increase in bending moments for loading condition (4.3), as opposed to the basic hypothesis of (4.1).

Axis 17: deck section at the anchorage of cable stays no. 9. This section experiences a reversal of bending moments.

From these results it is evident that the be-havior of the bridge changes dramatically under certain loading conditions and is prone to a varia-tion of 10% of the dead loads of the structure, which is similar in magnitude to the full live load of the bridge. The bridge was designed to with-stand the extreme bending moments calculated by the five hypotheses (4.1)–(4.5), and extreme cau-tion was exercised during construction to control the weights of the different pieces so that they would be as close as possible to the design values, and to keep an exact record of the bridge as built.

4.3
LIVE LOADS

Ten independent loading conditions in two groups were considered for live loads in the finite ele-ments analysis.

The first group consisted of two mutually exclusive loading conditions. First, the uniform 4 kPa live load was applied on the entire deck to produce a maximum gravity load. That loading condition developed large positive moments along the pylon as well as large moments on the steel box of the deck, and caused the bridge to deflect sub-stantially (fig. 4.4). Then the uniform 4 kPa live load was applied on only half of the deck, so it could produce a maximum torsion on the axis of the deck. The moment arm for such a load was equal to 8 m from the longitudinal axis of the bridge, with the moment arm increasing at the base of the pylon. That loading condition caused half the bending moments and deflection on the plane of the bridge of the full live load, but de-veloped a torsional moment along the steel box (fig. 4.5).

The second group of live loads consisted of eight mutually exclusive loading conditions, in which the truck load was applied on eight different locations along the deck: on nodes 6, 9, 15, 21, 27, 33, 39, and 45 of the model, corresponding to axes 44, 41, 35, 29, 23, 17, 11, and 5, respectively. The moment arm for the truck load at all locations is 13.30 m, which corresponds to the maximum pos-sible distance away from the steel box, thus devel-oping the maximum torsional moment. Among its possible locations, the 600 kN truck load on node 15 or axis 35, located 136 m from the east abut-

1.0DDL+1.0PDL+1.0CF   **1.0DDL+1.0PDL+0.9CF**   **1.0DDL+1.0PDL+1.1CF**

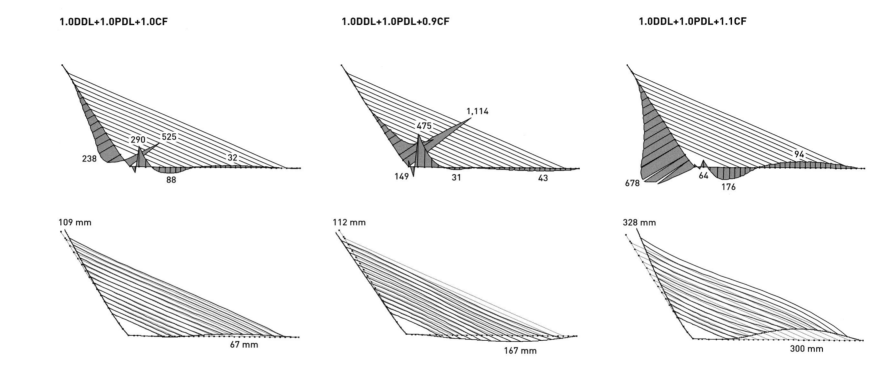

1.1DDL+0.9PDL+1.0CF

0.9DDL+1.1PDL+1.0CF

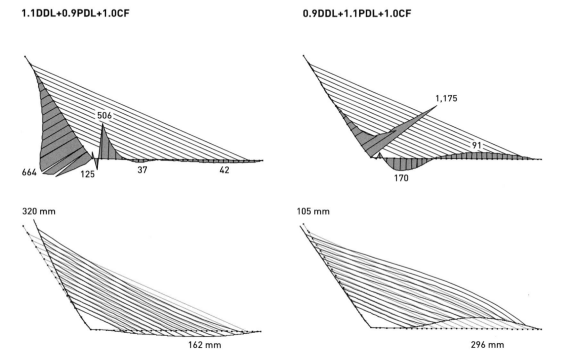

320 mm

105 mm

162 mm

296 mm

| **Fig. 4.2** | The bending moment diagrams (MN-m) and deflection diagrams of the bridge subject to the five variations of the dead and permanent loads. DDL: deck dead load; PDL: pylon dead load; CF: cable force. |

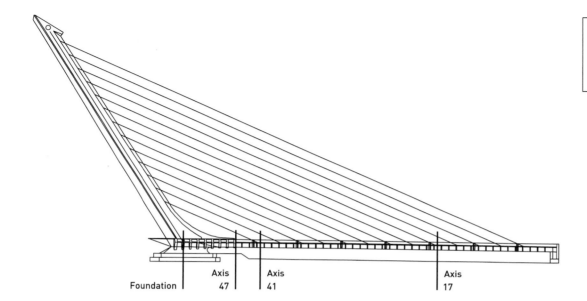

Axis
47

Axis
41

Axis
17

Foundation

Fig. 4.3 | The location of the four critical sections where the bending moments from the five variations of the dead and permanent loads are compared.

Table 4.8 The bending moments in MN-m at four critical sections, resulting from five hypotheses regarding the dead and permanent loads of the bridge. "Max" and "Min" refer to the maximum and minimum bending moments at each section, while "a" refers to the basic loading hypothesis (4.1) at each section.

	Loading condition (4.1)	Loading condition (4.2)	Loading condition (4.3)	Loading condition (4.4)	Loading condition (4.5)	$\frac{Max - a}{a}$	$\frac{Max - Min}{Min}$
Pile foundation	−525	−1,114	64	125	−1,175	1.2	10.4
Axis 47	−290	−475	0	−506	0	0.7	N/A
Axis 41	88	31	176	37	170	1.0	4.7
Axis 17	−32	43	−94	42	−91	1.8 and 2.3	3.2

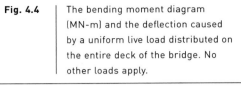

Fig. 4.4 The bending moment diagram (MN-m) and the deflection caused by a uniform live load distributed on the entire deck of the bridge. No other loads apply.

Fig. 4.5 The torsional moment diagram (MN-m) caused by a uniform live load distributed on half of the deck of the bridge. No other loads apply.

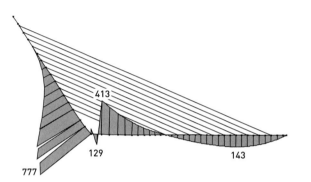

413

129

143

777

FULL LIVE LOAD

LIVE LOAD ON HALF THE DECK

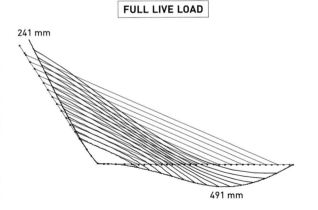

241 mm

491 mm

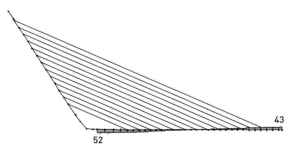

43

52

ment, proved to be the most critical for the deck of the bridge. The truck load itself developed very small bending moments on the pylon and the steel box; its effect was superimposed on the uniform live load and the other loads to obtain the design values for the structural elements of the bridge. The presence of the truck load was critical for the design of the local elements, such as the slab of the deck and the steel cantilevers.

4.4
THERMAL LOADS

Thermal loads result from the changing temperature of the elements of the bridge as a result of environmental conditions. The changing temperatures cause expansion or contraction of the materials that constitute the elements. If those elements are designed to expand or contract freely, then a change in temperature causes deformation but no stresses. When the free movements are constrained, however, stresses develop. As a statically indeterminate structure, the Alamillo Bridge experiences such stresses as a result of uniform temperature changes, in response to winter and summer conditions. The nature of the different materials, as well as their significant difference in mass, is expected to cause different expansion and

contraction in the cable stays, the pylon, and the deck. Furthermore, as a result of partial exposure to the sun, the temperature can gradually change within the mass of an element and reach extremes in opposite surfaces of the same element.

The variations in temperature of the main components of the Alamillo Bridge were calculated using a computer program of finite differences, solving numerically the partial differential equations that govern heat transfer within solids (tables 4.9 and 4.10). The input for such a program consists of the data describing maximum solar radiation in the summer and minimum solar radiation in the winter, the wind conditions at the site, the orientation of the structural elements and their size, and the thermal properties of steel and concrete.[4] Despite such extensive preconstruction analysis, site measurements during the first years of the bridge's life revealed that the temperature loads had been exaggerated during the design phase; the recorded temperature differences were significantly smaller than expected.[5]

Uniform changes in temperature either increase the tension of the cables or relax them partially. A temperature increase results in the elongation of a cable. The strain ε (change of length over the total length) that results from a change of temperature $\Delta\theta = 26°C$ for a steel cable

is:

$$\varepsilon = \frac{\Delta L}{L} = \alpha = \Delta\theta \rightarrow$$
$$\varepsilon = 12 \times (10^{-6})°C^{-1} \times 26°C \rightarrow$$
$$\varepsilon = 0.000312 \qquad (4.6)$$

where $\alpha = 12 \times (10^{-6})° C^{-1}$ is the thermal coefficient of steel.

For each cable of the twelve pairs with a modulus of elasticity $E = 200,000$ MPa and an area $A = 8,400$ mm², that strain corresponds to a change of force equal to:

$$\Delta F = \varepsilon \times E \times A \rightarrow$$
$$\Delta F = 0.000312 \times 200,000 \times 0.0084 \rightarrow$$
$$\Delta F = 0.524 \text{ MN} = 524 \text{ kN} \qquad (4.7)$$

Similarly, for each cable of the 13th pair with an area $A = 6,300$ mm², the change of force is:

$$\Delta F = \varepsilon \times E \times A \rightarrow$$
$$\Delta F = 0.000312 \times 200,000 \times 0.0063 \rightarrow$$
$$\Delta F = 0.393 \text{ MN} = 393 \text{ kN} \qquad (4.8)$$

The calculated changes of force correspond to approximately 10% of the post-tensioning force of the cables (see table 4.6).

Table 4.10 The daily variation in temperature within the body of the main structural elements. The cable stays do not experience any variation of temperature within their relatively small mass.

	Steel box		Completed deck	Pylon	
Summer	vertical	21.0°C	21°C	transverse	1.5°C
	horizontal	4.9°C		longitudinal	4.5°C
Winter	vertical	7.9°C	8°C	transverse	5.1°C
	horizontal	14.5°C		longitudinal	—
Design value*	vertical	21.0°C	21°C	transverse	5.1°C
	horizontal	14.5°C		longitudinal	4.5°C

*The vertical and horizontal variations in temperature should not apply simultaneously, nor should the transverse and longitudinal variations in temperature.

Table 4.9 Changes in temperature of the three main structural elements, treated as uniform across the element.

	Deck	Pylon	Cables
Summer	48.9°C	33.0°C	53.6°C
Winter	2.4°C	6.0°C	1.7°C
Design value	±23.3°C	±13.5°C	±26.0°C

According to expressions (4.6)–(4.8), all cables with the same cross-sectional area, regardless of their length, experience the same reduction of tension as a result of temperature increase. The longer cables will elongate more as a result of a temperature increase. However, long cables were also shortened more during their post-tensioning, and the change in elongation as a result of the temperature change has caused a proportional loss of that post-tensioning. This property makes it possible to use cables of significantly different lengths to support the deck of the bridge because, even under changing temperature, the change in the cable forces will be uniform along the deck.

Under a uniform rise in temperature, all elements expand. The pylon and the deck expand freely along their own longitudinal axes, as the pylon is free to expand and contract vertically and the deck is supported on the east abutment on neoprene. The elongation of the pylon and the deck causes, in turn, an elongation of the cables, which partially offsets the loss of tension as a result of the cables' own temperature increase. However, the higher temperature increase in the cables compared to the other elements, and the different orientation of the elements, lead to a partial loss of the post-tensioning in all the cables. Combined with a maximum live load, a temperature rise produces a

4 For more information, see the report of engineers Enrique Mirambell Arrizabaga and Angel C. Aparicio Bengoecha, "Establecimiento de las Acciones Térmicas a considerar en el Proyecto y Construcción del Puente Atirantado de Sevilla Paso del Alamillo," July 1989.

5 Technical Note 2.05, Fomento de Construcciones y Contratas SA, July 1993, p. 100.

critical load on the deck, since the pylon cannot take the full loads as the cables are loosened. Thus, the deck must carry more loads under such conditions, acting as a beam. On the other hand, a temperature rise combined with zero live load reduces the cables' support of the pylon, which must then rely more on its own fixed foundation.

Conversely, there is an increase in the force of the cables under a uniform drop in temperature, although such a uniform drop in temperature causes the pylon and the deck to contract and partially offset the increased tension of the cables. Combined with absence of live load, a temperature drop produces the most critical upward load for the deck and increases the load on the pylon, causing increased positive bending moments.

Although the cables are not affected by daily variations in temperature along their cross section, both the deck and the pylon experience such daily effects. The top surface of the deck is exposed to the sun throughout the day, while its lower surface is always in shade. According to an analysis of the bridge under these circumstances (table 4.10), that partial exposure to the sun is expected to produce a temperature difference of 21°C between the top surface and the lower surface of the deck. The pylon, on the other hand, because of its upright posi-

tion, is more uniformly exposed to the sun during different times of the day, and such differences in temperature are limited to 4.5°C on the plane of the bridge. These changes of temperature on opposite sides of the same element cause an expansion of the one side and a compression on the other. For freestanding elements, such changes cause deflections only, without generating stresses; but for the statically indeterminate Alamillo Bridge, such changes in strains cause a distortion of the geometry and load the structure. As the deck bends upward, accompanied by an inward movement of the pylon, the cables lose some of their tension. Thus, the pylon and the deck start to develop additional bending moments. Under high summer temperatures, such loss of tension can be amplified further.

The variation of the pylon's temperature in the transverse direction, which can reach 5.1°C according to the analysis, is quite a bit more complex, as it deforms the structure out of its plane of symmetry. The cable forces pull the pylon with an eccentricity, generating second-order bending moments and deflections.

Finite element analysis programs accept the temperature changes as input to predict the forces and stresses in a structure. These temperature changes are given both as uniform changes in tem-

perature and as a linearly changing temperature within the massive elements, specifying the temperature at the two opposite surfaces. Based on the values in tables 4.9 and 4.10, six independent loading cases were considered in the computer analysis model:

- 26°C change in the temperature of the cables,
- 13.5°C change in the temperature of the pylon,
- 23.3°C change in the temperature of the deck,
- 21°C gradient of temperature within the deck,
- 5.1°C gradient of temperature within the pylon, in the transverse direction,
- 4.5°C gradient of temperature within the pylon, in the longitudinal direction.

The finite element model showed that among the temperature variations and gradients, the change in the temperature of the cables alone caused the most significant bending moments in the bridge. Fig. 4.6 shows the bending moments and the deflection of the bridge resulting from a 26°C change in the temperature of the cables.

The six thermal loading cases were combined with the other loads acting on the structure to produce the most critical loading cases, as is described in section 4.8.

4.5
STATIC WIND LOADS

Spanish code OM/28-2-72 suggests using a maximum reference wind velocity of 50 m/sec and a 1.30 drag coefficient for all the elements of a structure. Furthermore, it suggests decreasing the loads during construction to 70% of the corresponding service loads. However, given the significance of the wind load on the Alamillo Bridge, the calculation of the anticipated wind forces was based on the data available at the Seville airport, administered by the Centro Meteorológico de Guadalquivir. Table 4.11 presents the design values adopted for the Alamillo Bridge, compared to the Spanish code OM/28-2-72, the British standard BS-5400, and the Swiss code SIA E160-1988.

A reference wind velocity of 170 km/h (47.22 m/sec) at a height of 6.80 m and at a suburban wind exposure was used for the loading of the

| **Fig. 4.6** | The bending moment diagram (MN-m) and the deflection caused by a 26°C temperature change in the cables of the bridge. No other loads apply. |

Table 4.11 A comparative study of wind forces based on international codes.

	Spanish OM/28-2-72	British BS-5400 1988	Swiss SIA E-160	Alamillo Bridge design values
Wind speed (m/sec)	50.00	50.00	40.80	47.20
C_D, deck	1.30	1.22	1.05	1.30
C_D, pylon	1.30	1.80	1.78	1.78
C_D, cables	1.30	0.70	1.20	1.20
Force on each element				
Deck (kN/m)	11.58	8.24	4.92	10.68
Pylon (at section 12, kN/m)	27.76	57.29	26.68	51.01
Pylon (at section 38, kN/m)	17.76	41.01	17.07	53.95
Cables (at deck level, kN/m)	0.78	0.67	0.51	0.67

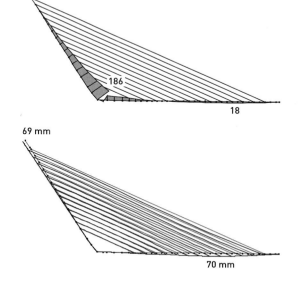

bridge. That wind velocity has a recurrence period of 500 years, based on a statistical analysis of the available data and assuming a Gumbel distribution. The wind velocity at a height y is given by the expression:

$$V(y) = C(y) \times V_{ref} \qquad (4.9)$$

$$\text{where } C(y) = \alpha \times \frac{\ln \dfrac{y}{0.30}}{\ln \dfrac{6.80}{0.07}} \qquad (4.10)$$

$$\text{so that } V(y) = (0.2513 \times \ln (y) + 0.3026) \times V_{ref} \qquad (4.11)$$

Expression (4.11), plotted next to the bridge in fig. 4.7, takes into account the difference in terrain between the suburban exposure of the airport and the rural site of the bridge, in the form of the coefficient $\alpha = 1.15$.

The maximum wind pressure on a structural element at a height y is calculated according to the maximum wind velocity at that height $V(y)$, the density of the air $\rho = 1.29$ kg/m^3, and the drag coefficient C_D.

Fig. 4.7 The 500-year wind velocity profile plotted next to the pylon of the Alamillo Bridge.

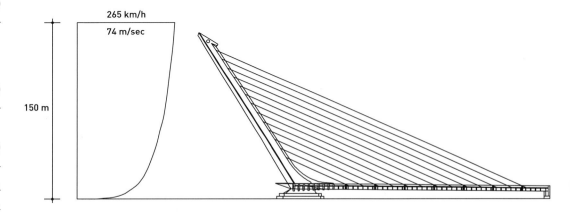

265 km/h
74 m/sec

150 m

$$p_w(y) = \frac{1}{2} \times \rho \times V^2 (y) \times C_D \qquad (4.12)$$

The drag coefficient C_D was estimated to be 1.30 for the deck, 1.78 for the pylon, and 1.20 for the cables. These estimates were derived based on the shape of those elements.

Thus, the design wind velocity for the deck, located at $y = 15$ m, was estimated to be 167 km/h (46.4 m/sec), yielding a wind pressure $p_w = 1.81$ kPa, corresponding to a force of 10.68 kN/m for the geometry of the deck as constructed. The wind pressure on the cables at the deck level was calculated to be $p_w = 1.67$ kPa, and the design wind force on the cables in their protective tubing was calcu-

Table 4.12 The wind forces on the nodes of the pylon.

Node (see fig. 4.8)	Pylon height y (m)	Wind velocity V (m/sec)	Pressure p_w (kPa)	Length of pylon cross section b_x (m)	Transverse force on pylon F_z (kN)	Width of pylon cross section b_z (m)	Longitudinal force on pylon F_x (kN)
51	142.400	73.1	6.15	7.00	199	8.00	228
49	133.154	72.3	6.02	9.20	456	8.06	399
46	125.952	71.7	5.91	9.20	392	8.14	347
43	118.750	71.0	5.80	9.56	399	8.22	343
40	111.534	70.2	5.68	9.90	407	8.30	341
37	104.278	69.4	5.55	10.25	410	8.38	336
34	97.097	68.6	5.41	10.58	412	8.48	331
31	89.876	67.7	5.27	10.95	418	8.56	327
28	82.594	66.7	5.11	11.30	417	8.64	319
25	75.430	65.6	4.95	11.65	415	8.74	311
22	68.205	64.4	4.77	12.00	413	8.82	304
19	60.997	63.1	4.58	12.40	408	8.92	294
16	53.824	61.6	4.36	12.75	399	9.00	282
13	46.653	59.9	4.13	13.10	389	9.08	270
10	39.439	57.9	3.86	13.48	426	9.14	289
7	30.272	54.8	3.45	14.97	413	9.28	256
4	23.453	51.7	3.08	17.73	456	9.36	241

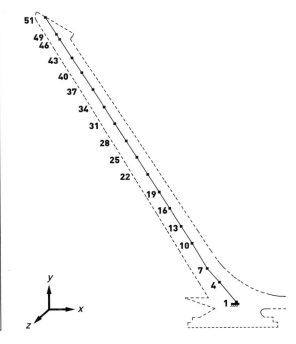

lated to be 667 N/m. The wind velocity, wind pressure, and the design forces on the pylon are given in table 4.12 (accompanied by fig. 4.8), for both the forces on the plane of the bridge and those perpendicular to it. Figs. 4.9 and 4.10 show the bending moments and the deflections of the bridge for wind load acting in the longitudinal and transverse directions. The horizontal loads on the deck that result from wind forces are taken by the steel box and the roadway slabs, which act together as a diaphragm. The uplifting forces on the deck are small compared to the weight of the deck and they are taken by the steel box.

Fig. 4.8 The pylon showing the finite element nodes.

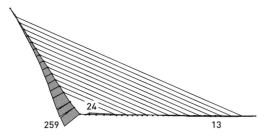

24

259

13

548

100 mm

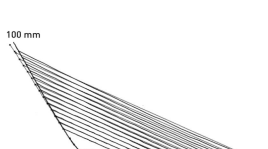

41 mm

281 mm

Fig. 4.9	The bending moment diagram (MN-m) and the deflection caused by wind along the direction of the bridge, toward the deck. No other loads apply.
Fig. 4.10	The bending moment diagram (MN-m) and the deflection caused by wind perpendicular to the axis of the bridge. No other loads apply.

4.6
DYNAMIC WIND LOADS

Static wind loads are based on a median wind velocity that generates a certain pressure on the surfaces of the structure. However, wind velocity is transient; changes in wind velocity, in the form of gusts, translate into eddies and turbulence. If the natural frequency of the structure is close to the frequency of the turbulence, then the loading from the turbulence could cause a dynamic excitation of the structure. Computer models predict the frequencies of the structures in different vibration modes. If those frequencies are close to the wind frequency, then a dynamic computer analysis is required. Alternatively, a dynamic amplification factor may be used to increase the static loads, in which case a pseudo-dynamic analysis can be performed. Wind tunnel tests also gauge the dynamic behavior of structures by simulating the effects of the surroundings. In addition, wind tunnel tests quite effectively measure the wind forces on various structural elements.

Calatrava insisted that the Alamillo Bridge was very stiff, having a high natural frequency, and that there should be no dynamic effects as a result of wind loading. He based his observation on the overall geometry and mass of the bridge. However,

Dragados y Construcciones SA proceeded with limited-scale wind tunnel tests performed on a model of the deck alone in order to study galloping and the effects of Von Karmann vortices. Based on those tests, the contractor advised the Junta de Andalucía to authorize wind tunnel tests on a complete model of the bridge in order to study the dynamic effects resulting from the interaction between the deck and the pylon.

In the spring of 1991, a 1:135 full aeroelastic model was constructed and tested in the boundary layer wind tunnel laboratory of the University of Western Ontario, Canada (King, Larose, and Davenport, 1991). The complete model of the bridge was made of aluminum, brass, acrylic, and vinyl (fig. 4.11) and was placed in the wind tunnel together with a complete model of the surroundings. The measured frequencies of the model, subject to the wind excitation, are given in table 4.13. These values are higher than the expected wind frequencies, as shown in fig. 4.12. The peaks in the wind spectrum occur near the frequency of 0.017 Hz

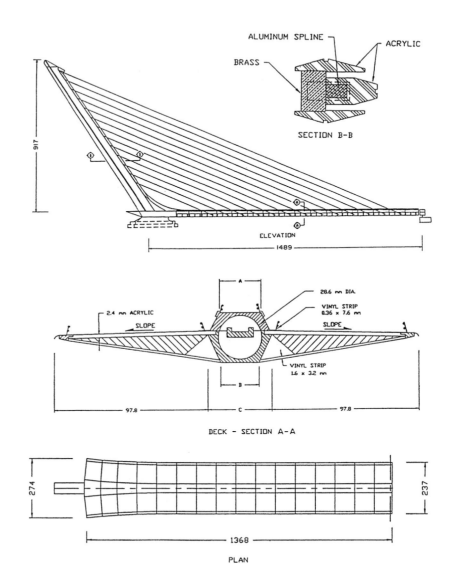

| **Fig. 4.11** | The drawings of the 1:135 full aeroelastic model that was tested in the wind tunnel for its dynamic behavior. |

Table 4.13 Frequencies of the structural elements of the bridge.

Deck		
Lift mode	1st:	0.373 Hz
	2nd:	1.191 Hz
Drag mode	1st:	1.088 Hz
	2nd:	3.244 Hz
Torque mode	1st:	1.235 Hz
	2nd:	2.311 Hz
Pylon		
Parallel to the wind	1st:	0.292 Hz
	2nd:	1.583 Hz
Transverse to the wind	1st:	0.373 Hz
	2nd:	0.610 Hz
	3rd:	2.1969 Hz

Fig. 4.12 | A typical wind spectrum and the frequencies of the natural modes of the Alamillo Bridge.

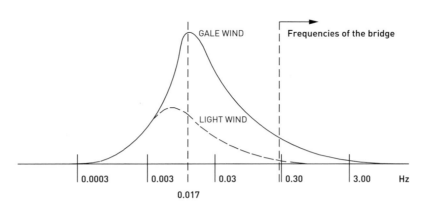

(period $T = 1$ min), and the wind energy diminishes in the higher frequencies of more than 0.10 Hz (period $T = 10$ sec), where most structures have their natural frequencies (Davenport, 1970).

A lower turbulence (6% intensity of turbulence) was used to study the generation of vortices and other dynamic instabilities, while a higher turbulence (24% intensity of turbulence at the deck level, at a height $y_0 = 0.30$ m) was used to study extreme wind forces. The model had a variable structural damping ranging from 0.25% to 0.75%, less than the damping expected in the actual structure and less than the damping encountered in most bridges of a similar type and size, whose average damping is 0.90%. The reduced damping ensured conservative results from the dynamic tests.

Buffeting prevailed among the observed dynamic effects, but there was no rapid increase in the dynamic response of the model for median wind velocities up to 90 m/sec at the deck level. Furthermore, the model response was proportional to the intensity of the turbulence. Thus, the wind tunnel simulation demonstrated that there is no dynamic amplification as a result of turbulence-induced vibrations, and that the wind loads that had been calculated based on static considerations alone should be used for the design.

4.7
SEISMIC LOADS

Two load cases were considered for seismic loads: horizontal seismic loads acting on the plane of the bridge, and horizontal seismic loads acting perpendicular to the bridge. They were applied as uniform loads on the pylon only, and their magnitude was the same for either direction. According to the applicable Spanish code, the magnitude of each horizontal load was 3% of the weight of the corresponding segment of the pylon.

The seismic loads on the pylon were smaller than the maximum wind loads (table 4.14). Given that the wind load corresponds to the 500-year extreme and the seismic load has a similar recurrence, it was safe to assume that the structure might be subject either to wind loads or to seismic loads alone but not to both at once. This being the case, static wind loads provide a more critical loading case.

4.8
LOAD COMBINATIONS

Three different load combinations were used to determine the dimensions of the various elements

Table 4.14 A comparison between the seismic loads and the wind loads on the pylon of the bridge.

Node	Height y (m)	Wind F_z (kN)	Wind F_x (kN)	Seismic F_z and F_x (kN)
51	142.400	199	228	144
49	133.154	456	399	180
46	125.952	392	347	165
43	118.750	399	343	264
40	111.534	407	341	278
37	104.278	410	336	293
34	97.097	412	331	308
31	89.876	418	327	323
28	82.594	417	319	338
25	75.430	415	311	325
22	68.205	413	304	312
19	60.997	408	294	327
16	53.824	399	282	343
13	46.653	389	270	360
10	39.439	426	289	486
7	30.272	413	256	508
4	23.453	456	241	537

of the bridge. The combinations were used for an ultimate-strength design, so they were increased by the corresponding amplification factors.

$$1.5 \times \text{dead loads} + 1.5 \times \text{live loads} \qquad (4.13)$$

$$0.90 \times (1.5 \times \text{dead loads} + 1.5 \times \text{live loads}) + 1.35 \times \text{wind} + \text{thermal} \qquad (4.14)$$

$$0.80 \times (1.5 \times \text{dead loads} + 1.5 \times \text{live loads}) + \text{seismic loads} + \text{wind during an earthquake} \qquad (4.15)$$

Dead loads: The most critical forces for each element were derived from the five combinations of the dead and permanent loads, as described by expressions (4.1)–(4.5), to reflect construction tolerances.

Live loads: This includes the uniform load of 4 kPa, plus the 600 kN truck load at the most critical location for every structural element.

Wind loads: The wind loads result from the wind acting either on the plane of the bridge or perpendicular to the plane of the bridge.

Thermal loads: The thermal loads are generated either by uniform temperature variations or by variations in temperature within the structural elements. For the pylon, the variation in tempera-

ture may be either within the plane of the bridge or perpendicular to the plane of the bridge.

Seismic loads: The seismic loads act on the pylon either on the plane of the bridge or perpendicular to the plane of the bridge.

Fig. 4.13 shows the five most critical load combinations. The values of the bending moments on the plots include the amplification factors for the ultimate-strength design, while the values of the corresponding deflections do not include any amplification factors.

Load combination *A* corresponds to the loading condition given by expression (4.13), with the assumption that the bridge is loaded with the maximum live loads. The uniform live load applies on the entire deck; the truck load is located on node 15. The dead load of the deck is increased by 10% and the dead load of the pylon is decreased by 10% in order to develop cumulative effects with the live load.

Load combinations *B*, *C*, *D*, and *E* correspond to the loading condition given by expression (4.14). Load combination *B* assumes that the live load is applied on the entire deck; the truck load is again located on node 15 and wind blows in the longitudinal direction toward the deck (eastbound). On a cold day, the pylon, the deck, and the cables can be assumed to be as cold as possible,

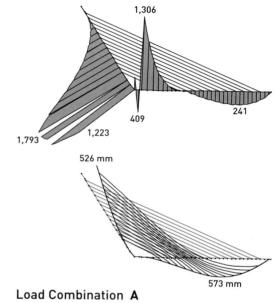

Load Combination A

and the thermal gradient for the pylon makes it curve toward the deck, so that the loads have cumulative effects. The dead load of the deck is increased by 10% and the dead load of the pylon is decreased by 10%. Load combination *C* is the same as *B* except that it assumes warm weather conditions, so the thermal loads act in the opposite direction from load combination *B*.

Load combination *D* assumes that the bridge has no live loads. The wind blows west-

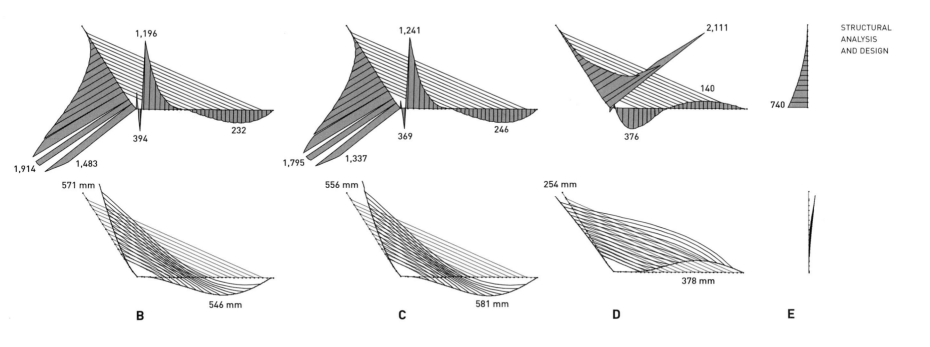

1,196

1,241

2,111

140

740

232

394

246

369

376

1,914

1,483

1,795

1,337

571 mm

556 mm

254 mm

546 mm

581 mm

378 mm

B

C

D

E

Fig. 4.13 The bending moment diagrams (MN-m) and the deflections caused by the most extreme loading conditions. The magnitudes of the bending moments include the corresponding amplification factors for the ultimate-strength analysis. The deflections do not include any amplification factors. See text for a description of the load combinations.

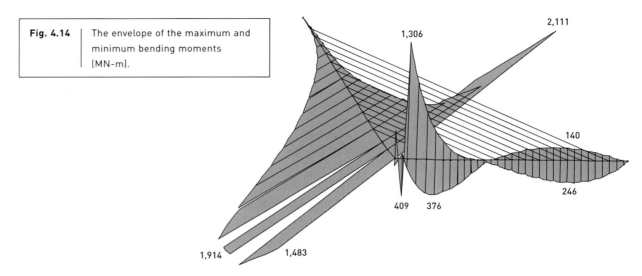

Fig. 4.14 | The envelope of the maximum and minimum bending moments (MN-m).

bound and the thermal loads correspond to a warm day, so the pylon, the deck, and the cables expand. The thermal gradient for the pylon makes it bend away from the deck. The dead load of the deck is decreased by 10% and the dead load of the pylon is increased by 10%.

Load combination E assumes transverse wind and transverse thermal gradient for the pylon. The live loads on the bridge generate second-order effects.

The loading condition given by expression (4.15) does not produce critical loads for the bridge, since the seismic loads are smaller than the wind loads on the pylon.

Fig. 4.14 shows the envelopes of the maximum and minimum bending moments on the bridge, both on the plane of the bridge and the transverse direction. Such bending moment diagrams were produced for all possible load combinations and second-order effects to which the bridge might be subjected.

4.9
DESIGN OF THE STRUCTURAL ELEMENTS

The concrete elements of the bridge were designed by Carlos Alonso-Cobo, Professor of Reinforced Concrete Structures in the School of Civil Engineering in Santander.[6] They included the pedestal, the pylon, the roadway slabs, and the abutments. José Ramón Atienza-Reales, Professor of Structures and Steel Bridges at the School of Civil Engineering of the Technical University of Valencia,[7] designed the steel elements of the bridge, i.e., the torsion box and the cantilevering wings.

The finite element analysis determined the maximum and minimum forces and moments that act on each structural member of the bridge under the specified loading combinations. Those forces and moments were used to determine whether the selected sections of the elements that were part of the input for the finite element analysis were sufficient to withstand the loads, and would deflect within the allowable limits. For the concrete members, the focus was on determining the appropriate reinforcement and whether that reinforcement would be within reason. For the steel elements, the goal was to determine whether the strength and stiffness were sufficient.

The results converged after a few iterations, i.e., the cross-sectional shapes were sufficient and appropriate to withstand the calculated loads, and they conformed to the overall deflection requirements. Those sections are presented in the selected construction drawings in appendix C; their properties have been described in tables 4.1 and 4.2.

The consideration of variations in the dead and permanent loads (see section 4.2) introduced amplification factors for the ultimate-strength design that exceeded those of the load combinations outlined in section 4.8. So, after the structural members of the bridge were designed, a reverse analysis was performed to identify the actual margin of safety that had been introduced in the design. This process provided further reassurance as to the future behavior of the bridge.

The coefficients γ_1, γ_2, γ_3, γ_4, and γ_5 were determined for five different hypotheses:

$$(0.90\ W_{pylon} + 1.15\ W_{deck}) + T_{cables} + \gamma_1 \times (q + Q + W_x) \tag{4.16}$$

$$(0.90\ W_{pylon} + 1.15\ W_{deck}) + T_{cables} + \Delta T_y + \gamma_2 \times (q + Q + W_y) \tag{4.17}$$

$$(1.35\ W_{pylon} + 1.35\ W_{deck}) + T_{cables} + \gamma_3 \times (q + Q + W_x) \tag{4.18}$$

$$(1.35\ W_{pylon} + 1.35\ W_{deck}) + T_{cables} + \Delta T + \gamma_4 \times (q + Q + W_y) \tag{4.19}$$

$$(1.15\ W_{pylon} + 0.90\ W_{deck}) + T_{cables} + \gamma_5 \times (-W_x) \tag{4.20}$$

where q is the uniform live load, Q the concentrated load from the truck, W_x the wind load on the plane of the bridge, W_y the wind load perpendicular to the plane of the bridge, and ΔT the thermal load.

The loads were applied in steps, in a computer program using nonlinear analysis:

step I = dead and permanent loads + tension of the cables,

step II = I + uniform load on the entire deck +

truck load at node 15 (if applicable),

step III = II + wind longitudinal or transversal, depending on hypothesis,

step IV = III + thermal variation (if applicable),

step V = IV + deviation from permanent weights (i.e., $-0.10\,W_{pylon}$ and $0.15\,W_{deck}$; or $0.35\,W_{pylon}$ and $0.35\,W_{deck}$; or $0.15\,W_{pylon}$ and $-0.10\,W_{deck}$, according to the hypotheses),

step VI = V + increase 20% of both live and wind loads,

step VII = VI + increase 20% of both live and wind loads,

step VIII = VII + increase 20% of both live and wind loads.

6 Profesor en la Cátedra de Estructuras de Hormigón Armado de la Escuela Técnica Superior de Ingenieros de Caminos, Canales y Puertos de Santander.

7 Catedrático de Estructura y Puentes Metálicos de la Escuela Técnica Superior de Ingenieros de Caminos y Puentes de la Universidad Politécnica de Valencia.

Subsequent steps increased the live and wind loads by 20% until the structure reached its ultimate strength. At that point, the coefficient γ_ι was determined. The process was repeated five times to determine the five coefficients.

According to the analyses, the magnitudes of the coefficients were satisfactory, calculated to be:

$$\gamma_1 = 2.0 \qquad (4.21)$$

$$\gamma_2 = 2.0 \qquad (4.22)$$

$\gamma_3 \geq 1.4$, the analysis was interrupted because of numerical problems at $\gamma_3 = 1.4$, which provides a sufficient margin of safety. $\qquad (4.23)$

$\gamma_4 \geq 1.4$, the analysis was interrupted because of numerical problems at $\gamma_4 = 1.4$, which provides a sufficient margin of safety. $\qquad (4.24)$

$\gamma_5 \geq 3.0$, the analysis was terminated at $\gamma_5 = 3.0$, which provides a sufficient margin of safety. $\qquad (4.25)$

The finite element analysis indicated that the variation in the forces of the cable stays are unusually low for a cable-stayed bridge. The variation between maximum and minimum tensile forces is largest in the cables that support the middle of the deck (4th to 8th pair of cables), and those variations are limited to ±10% of the average value. The cables were designed to support the deck in pairs to allow their future replacement (see section 6.5.4 for cable replacement).

4.10
DESIGN OF THE FOUNDATION

The foundation was designed by Carlos Alonso-Cobo as well. The loads at the foundation were determined from the finite element analysis of the bridge. All possible load combinations were considered, and the reactions at the foundation of the pylon were two orders of magnitude higher than the reactions at the east abutment (a hypothesis that was presented in section 3.1.4). The following two cases were the most critical for the foundation of the pylon:

(dead + permanent loads) + live loads
+ longitudinal wind $\qquad (4.26)$

(dead + permanent loads) + live loads
+ transverse wind $\qquad (4.27)$

Table 4.15 gives the design values of the axial force and the bending moments for the foundation of the pylon. These values do not include any amplification factors, since the safety coefficients are introduced later in the allowable stresses of the soil. The 175 MN weight of the pedestal and the pile cap is included in the design values, as well as a 86.8 MN-m moment generated by the eccentricity of that weight on the plane of the bridge. The bending moment in the transverse direction was increased following a second-order analysis. Subject to transverse wind loading, the pylon deflects laterally, and that deflection creates additional

Table 4.15 The maximum loads acting on the foundation.

Load case	Axial force (MN)	Transverse moment (MN-m)	Longitudinal moment (MN-m)
(4.1)	427	0	2,180
(4.2)	427	683	1,846

bending moments from the developed eccentricity of its own weight and the forces from the cables. That second-order bending moment was calculated to be equal to 24% of the moment generated by the transverse wind, reaching 683 MN-m.

4.10.1
SOIL PROFILE

The soil borings and studies for the soil profile were carried out by Laboratorio Analisis Industriales VORSEVI SA. Fig. 4.15 shows the data from several borings at the vicinity of the foundation of the pylon. After 3 m of organic material, there is a 9 m deep layer of fine sand containing some clay, which makes it behave like coarse silt. The next 6 m, down to a depth of 18 m, consist of gray sand mixed with some gravel, followed by 8 m of gravel with some sand. At 26 m, a stratum of gray marl begins.

The experimental values of N_{SPT} (standard penetration test) for the top layers, and the ultimate uniaxial strength q_u for the marl, are plotted at left

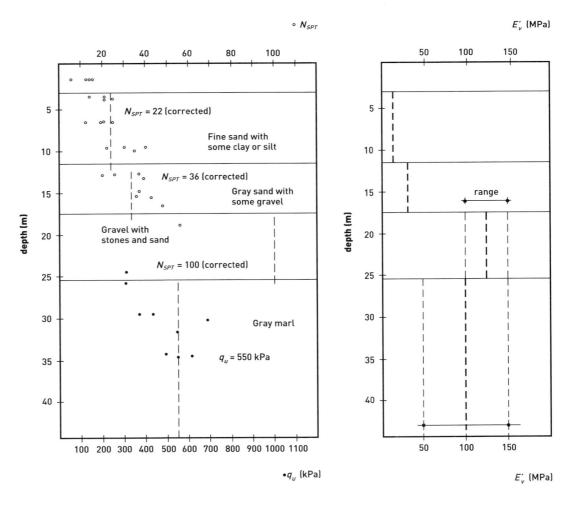

Fig. 4.15 The soil profile and the data from the borings. See text.

in fig. 4.15. The dotted lines indicate the design values, summarized in table 4.16.

4.10.2
DESIGN OF THE PILES

An early design proposed a series of rectangular piers embedded in the sand and gravel, bearing on the marl. However, such a design provided insufficient stiffness for rotation under the anticipated bending moments at the foundation of the pylon. Thus the rectangular piers were substituted with piles 2 m in diameter embedded in the marl. A group of 54 end-bearing reinforced concrete bored piles constitutes the foundation of the pylon; their coordinates are given in table 4.17.

Table 4.16 The design values for N_{SPT} and q_u.

Depth	Design values
3–12 m	$N_{SPT} = 22$ (corrected)
12–18 m	$N_{SPT} = 36$ (corrected)
18–26 m	$N_{SPT} = 100$ (corrected)
>26 m	$q_u = 550$ kPa

The bearing capacity P_b of a single pile with an area $A_b = 3.14 m^2$, resting on marl, was calculated to be:

$$P_b = 9 \times \frac{1}{2} q_u \times A_b = 7.6 \text{ MN} \qquad (4.28)$$

The friction along the pile shaft in the granular material was calculated from the most conservative results for the unit shaft friction (τ_f). This is related to the corrected standard penetration number (N_{SPT}) and the constituency of the soil layers, calculated as:

3–12 m	$N_{SPT} = 22$	$\tau_f = 13.0$ kPa
12–18 m	$N_{SPT} = 36$	$\tau_f = 28.8$ kPa
18–26 m	$N_{SPT} = 100$	$\tau_f = 80.0$ kPa (4.29)

The shaft friction in the marl is based on the undrained shear strength ($c_u = 0.5q_u$), using a correlation coefficient α ranging from 0.33 to 1.33. A conservative estimate, calculated not to exceed $\tau_f = 100$ kPa, suggests that $\alpha = 0.36$.

$$\tau_f = \alpha \times c_u = 0.36 \times 275 = 100 \text{ kPa} \qquad (4.30)$$

Such an estimate is justified by the presence of a weaker layer of 2 to 3 m on top of the marl stratum,

with $q_u = 350$ kPa, instead of the design value of $q_u = 550$ kPa in the main body of the marl.

Based on the above values, the pile shaft friction of a single pile in the granular stratum is 5,611 kN. The total pile shaft friction depends on the length L of the pile embedded in the marl:

$$P_s = 5,611 + 616 \times L \qquad (4.31)$$

For the design loads of table 4.15 and the coordinates of the piles as given in table 4.17, the largest axial load in any pile is 12.81 MN. After incorporating the recommended safety factors for a large bored pile, the required length of the pile in marl is calculated:

$$\frac{1}{3} P_b + \frac{1}{2} P_s = 12.81 \text{ MN} \rightarrow L = 24 \text{ m} \qquad (4.32)$$

Later studies during the construction of the bridge showed that the maximum axial load on a single pile may reach 14.22 MN. This new figure resulted from an updated estimate of the expected forces and moments on the foundation, as a result of the actual weight of the structural elements and the pedestal. However, the newly incorporated safety factors and the conservative estimates of the soil properties prevented any concern.

Table 4.17 The coordinates of the piles (see fig. 6.3).

Pile	x	y	Pile	x	y
1	−12.00	12.00	28	−4.00	−11.43
2	−8.00	11.71	29	0.00	−11.14
3	−4.00	11.43	30	4.00	−10.86
4	0.00	11.14	31	8.00	−10.57
5	4.00	10.86	32	12.00	−10.29
6	8.00	10.57	33	16.00	−10.00
7	12.00	10.29	34	−14.00	−8.50
8	16.00	10.00	35	−10.00	−8.20
9	−14.00	8.50	36	−5.98	−7.87
10	−10.00	8.20	37	−1.97	−7.53
11	−5.98	7.87	38	2.05	−7.20
12	−1.97	7.53	39	6.07	−6.87
13	2.05	7.20	40	10.08	−6.53
14	6.07	6.87	41	14.10	−6.20
15	10.08	6.53	42	18.00	−5.00
16	14.10	6.20	43	−16.00	−5.00
17	18.00	5.00	44	−12.00	−4.60
18	−16.00	5.00	45	−7.50	−4.15
19	−12.00	4.60	46	−3.00	−3.70
20	−7.50	4.15	47	1.50	−3.25
21	−3.00	3.70	48	6.00	−2.80
22	1.50	3.25	49	10.00	−2.40
23	6.00	2.80	50	14.00	−2.00
24	10.00	2.40	51	−16.00	0.00
25	14.00	2.00	52	−12.00	0.00
26	−12.00	−12.00	53	−7.50	0.00
27	−8.00	−11.71	54	18.00	0.00

The group of piles is connected with a pile cap embedded in the sand, consisting of a solid concrete block 28 m by 38 m and 4.5 m deep. The group action for the average load on each pile yields a safety coefficient of 2.13 for a total load of 427 MN. This calculation assumes a group efficiency coefficient of 0.60, reflecting the proximity of the piles to each other.

4.10.3
SETTLEMENT AND ROTATION

The settlement of the pile group was estimated not to exceed 70 mm, based on the following properties of the soil (see fig. 4.15, right):

for 3–12 m,	$E_v = 13$ MPa
for 12–18 m,	$E_v = 28$ MPa
for 18–26 m,	$E_v = 100$ MPa
for 26+ m,	$E_v = 36$ MPa

(most conservative in literature, derived as

$$E_v = 130\ c_u) \tag{4.33}$$

Special care was taken to determine the rotation of the foundation subject to the anticipated bending moments. After a detailed calculation of the horizontal resistance of the foundation according to Terzaghi (1955), the rotation of the foundation was studied based on a solid block 37 m long, 26 m wide, and 45.5 m deep (fig. 4.16). Taking into account the properties of the different soil layers, the rotation was calculated to be less than 0.06° on the plane of the bridge. Following similar considerations, the transversal rotation of the foundation subject to the maximum transverse bending moment was found to be less than 0.026°.

Following those calculations, a design value of 0.25% (0.225°) was selected for a rotation of the base of the pylon on the plane of the bridge, which is 3.75 times higher than the calculated value. The 0.25% rotation of the base of the pylon corresponds to a 500 mm differential settlement between the base of the pylon and the east abutment. Similarly, the design value of 0.10% (0.09°) was selected for rotation out of the plane of the bridge, which is 3.5 times higher than the calculated value.

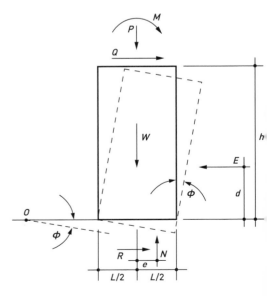

Fig. 4.16 | Calculations of the rotation of the foundation assuming a rigid block behavior.

5 CONSTRUCTION PLANNING

The design of the Alamillo Bridge required unprecedented precision in construction, with very low tolerances in the weights and the positioning of the various elements. During design, every decision related to structural engineering was tested for its construction feasibility as well. Based on engineering considerations, a tight construction schedule was established and was followed precisely throughout the construction operations. Detailed records and extensive instrumentation provided the required information during construction and feedback on the validity of the assumptions, the accuracy of operations, and margins for error. Repeated computer-based analyses were required at every stage of construction, taking into account the actual weights and the exact geometry of the recently completed elements.

5.1
INITIAL CONSTRUCTION SCHEDULE

As part of the initial conception of the bridge with its single inclined pylon, Calatrava had envisioned a simultaneous cantilevering construction of the pylon and the deck, starting from the Cartuja side. That construction plan formed part of the bidding documents, and was adhered to during the early design development stage.

The bidding documents showed the foundation consisting of 90 piers, 2.5 m by 0.8 m each, with their long axis perpendicular to the axis of the bridge, reaching at the top of the marl at a depth of 18.5 m. The steel box would be prefabricated and transported in segments of 4 m, three of which would be welded on the site to make segments 12 m long (fig. 5.1, top center). The segments would be raised to cantilever ahead the box and then attach the steel wings and the roadway. Each of those 12 m segments corresponded to a single pair of cables. Finally, the pylon was designed to be constructed with a sliding formwork in two steps for each segment, corresponding to a single pair of cables. Each pair of the then 17 pairs of the cable stays would be post-tensioned after the corresponding segments of the deck and the pylon had been constructed. The protective material in the cables would be injected into all the casings of the cables together toward the end of construction.

According to the schedule used for bidding (fig. 5.1), the construction was estimated to take 24 months. The construction of the piers for the pylon foundation was scheduled to last 4.5 months, with an additional 1.5 months for the piers of the abutment on the Seville side. The lower part of the pylon was scheduled to last 6.5 months, with 2 additional months for the abutment on the Seville side.

Construction of each 12 m segment of the deck, including the assembly of the steel box and the cantilevering wings and placement of the concrete slab for the roadway, would take three weeks. Within that time, the corresponding segment of pylon was scheduled to be constructed in two stages, each approximately 3.6 m high, with three days for preparing the sliding formwork, four days for positioning the reinforcement, and one day for placing the concrete. The 24th month was reserved for finishing work and for load-testing the bridge.

5.2
REVISED CONSTRUCTION SCHEDULE

The initial schedule was not feasible. Its major flaw was the requirement for simultaneous completion of the various distinct and fundamentally different components of the deck—which was intended to ensure the weight necessary to balance the corresponding segment of the pylon—as well as the requirement for a tight coordination between the construction of the pylon and the construction of the deck.

After bidding, the construction companies revised the schedule (fig. 5.2). The new schedule was based on the same design information as dictated the original schedule, and it was to take only one month longer. However, it divided the construction of the deck from the construction of the pylon and proposed to support the deck during construction at three temporary stations on the riverbed. Thus, construction of the steel box could proceed at two 12 m segments per week. The assembly of the roadways would follow, starting from the pylon side. At the same time, the pylon would be constructed in segments 3.6 m high, with each segment planned to take 1.5 weeks, as in the initial schedule. According to the revised schedule, the bridge would be completed by September 1991.

5.3
ACTUAL CONSTRUCTION SCHEDULE

The contractors changed substantially the construction process following the modifications that resulted from design development. The new plan reflected the need to complete construction in a shorter overall time, after valuable time had been diverted to design development and the construc-

Fig. 5.1 | Initial schedule for the construction of the bridge, part of the bidding documents, graphically applied to the profile of the bridge.

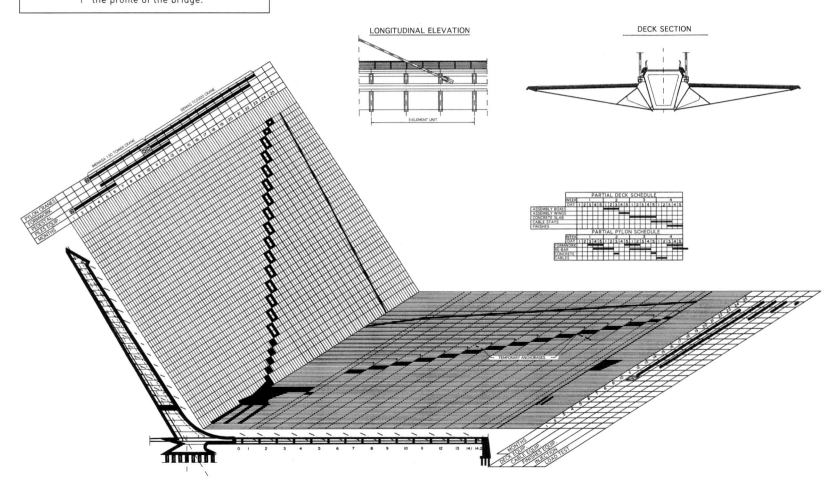

LONGITUDINAL ELEVATION

3-ELEMENT UNIT

DECK SECTION

PARTIAL DECK SCHEDULE

PARTIAL PYLON SCHEDULE

TEMPORARY ANCHORAGES

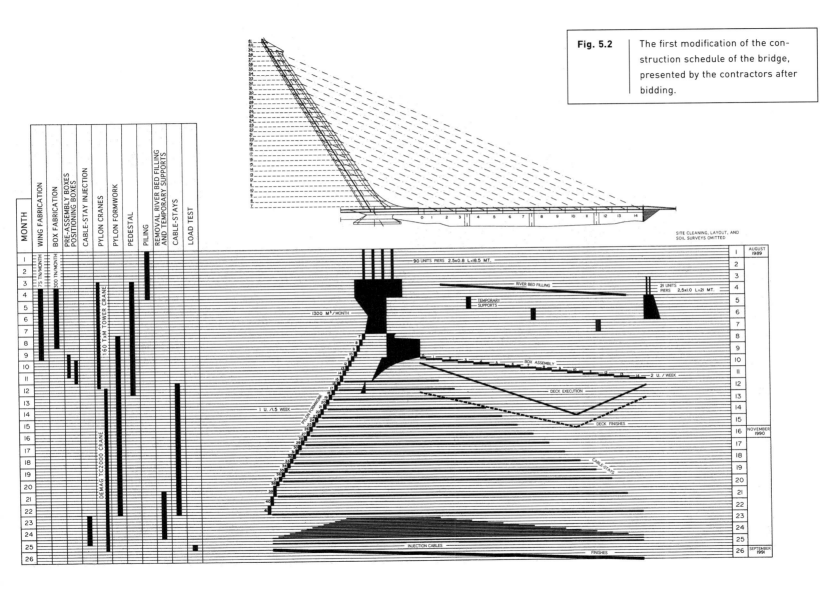

Fig. 5.2 The first modification of the construction schedule of the bridge, presented by the contractors after bidding.

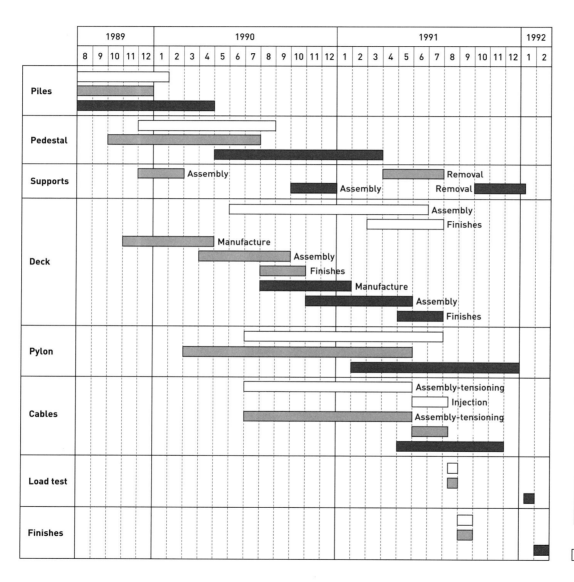

tion of the pylon's foundation. According to the new plan, the construction of the deck was completely uncoupled from the construction of the pylon, requiring seven temporary supports for the deck. Steel caissons would be used for the construction of the pylon, a significant change from the original plan. If prefabricated steel caissons were used, the construction time of each segment of the pylon would be reduced to 2 weeks instead of 3 as in the previous schedules, which were based on the use of sliding formwork. This time saving was due to the prefabrication of the steel caissons, the need for less steel reinforcement for the enclosed concrete, and the less complicated process of filling the caissons with concrete. Finally, the selection of epoxy-coated strands from which to assemble the cables in situ allowed a more flexible schedule and did not impose time limits on applying a corrosion protection during construction.

Fig. 5.3 | The actual construction schedule of the bridge compared to the initial bidding schedule and the first modified schedule, based on six-day work weeks.

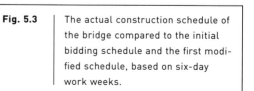

☐ Bid (fig. 5.1)   ▨ Planned (fig. 5.2)   ■ Actual

AVERAGE CABLE STAY ASSEMBLY CYCLE   ■ Left cable stay   ■ Right cable stay   ■ Both cable stays   [6] No. of workers

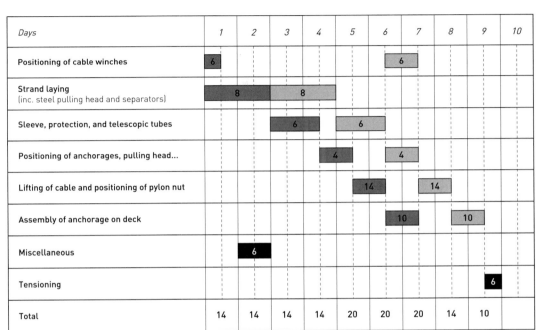

Days	1	2	3	4	5	6	7	8	9	10
Positioning of cable winches	6					6				
Strand laying (inc. steel pulling head and separators)	8	8								
Sleeve, protection, and telescopic tubes			6	6						
Positioning of anchorages, pulling head…				4		4				
Lifting of cable and positioning of pylon nut						14	14			
Assembly of anchorage on deck						10		10		
Miscellaneous		6								
Tensioning									6	
Total	14	14	14	14	20	20	20	14	10	

Fig. 5.4 | The actual schedule for assembly, installation, tensioning, and grouting the end of the cable stays. The numbers indicate numbers of workers engaged on each operation.

The actual construction schedule for the bridge, compared to the original and modified schedules (fig. 5.3), shows the delay in constructing the foundation of the pylon, the late start on and lengthy process of building the pedestal and the deck, and the significant time savings for both the construction of the pylon and the installation of the cables.

The actual assembly, installation, tensioning, and grouting the end of the cable stays took an average of 9 working days per pair of cables and required an average crew of 16 workers (fig. 5.4).

The stages of the construction of the bridge are shown in figs. 5.5 and 5.6, with the actual dates of construction for each task.

Stage 1

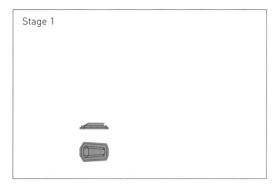

construction of foundation and pedestal

Stage 2

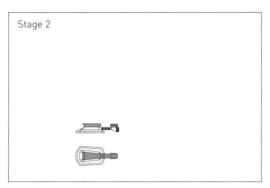

construction of concrete part of the torsion box
31-Oct-90   assembly of 1st caisson for steel box

Stage 3

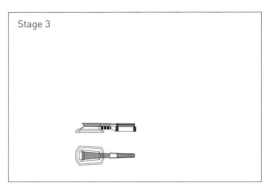

23-Nov-90   assembly of 2nd caisson for steel box;
further work on pedestal

Stage 4

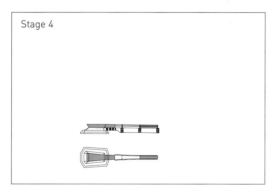

13-Dec-90   assembly of 3rd caisson for steel box;
further work on pedestal

Stage 5

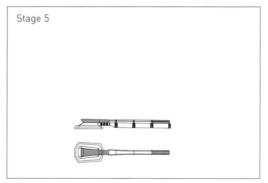

26-Dec-90   assembly of 4th caisson for steel box;
further work on pedestal

Stage 6

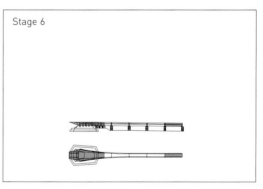

20-Jan-91   assembly of 5th caisson for steel box;
further work on pedestal

Fig. 5.5 | The first 12 of the 24 stages of the construction of the bridge. Activities shown in gray on plan
and elevation.

Stage 7

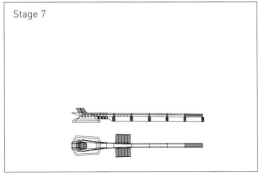

13-Jan-91 placement of concrete slab along 2nd caisson
of the deck
05-Feb-91 assembly of 1st caisson of pylon
06-Feb-91 assembly of 6th caisson for steel box

Stage 8

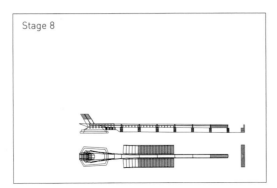

27-Feb-91 assembly of 2nd caisson of pylon
01-Mar-91 assembly of 7th caisson for steel box
04-Mar-91 placement of concrete slab along 3rd and 4th
caissons of deck

Stage 9

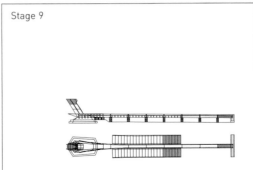

22-Mar-91 assembly of 8th caisson for steel box
01-Apr-91 assembly of 3rd caisson of pylon
03-Apr-91 placement of concrete slab along 5th caisson
of deck

Stage 10

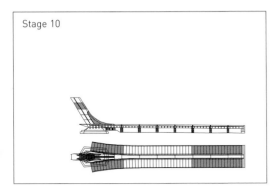

09-May-91 placement of concrete slab inside 4th caisson
of pylon
18-May-91 assembly of 5th caisson of pylon
21-May-91 placement of concrete for remainder of deck

Stage 11

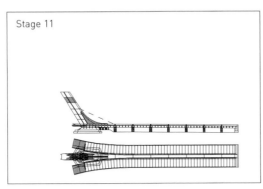

24-May-91 post-tension of cable stays no. 1
29-May-91 placement of concrete inside 5th caisson of pylon
31-May-91 assembly of 6th caisson of pylon

Stage 12

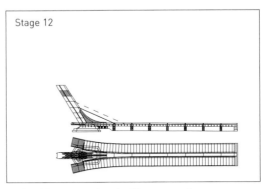

10-Jun-91 post-tension of cable stays no. 2
12-Jun-91 placement of concrete inside 6th caisson of pylon
13-Jun-91 assembly of 7th caisson of pylon

Stage 13

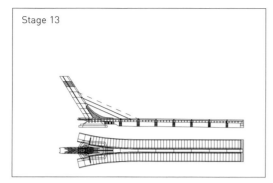

22-Jun-91 post-tension of cable stays no. 3
24-Jun-91 placement of concrete inside 7th caisson of pylon
26-Jun-91 assembly of 8th caisson of pylon

Stage 14

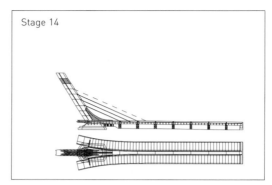

06-Jul-91 post-tension of cable stays no. 4
09-Jul-91 placement of concrete inside 8th caisson of pylon
10-Jul-91 assembly of 9th caisson of pylon

Stage 15

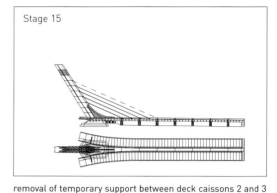

removal of temporary support between deck caissons 2 and 3
20-Jul-91 post-tension of cable stays no. 5
23-Jul-91 placement of concrete inside 9th caisson of pylon
24-Jul-91 assembly of 10th caisson of pylon

Stage 16

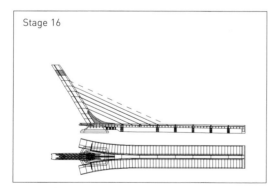

removal of temporary support between deck caissons 3 and 4
20-Jul-91 post-tension of cable stays no. 6
23-Jul-91 placement of concrete inside 10th caisson of pylon
24-Jul-91 assembly of 11th caisson of pylon

Stage 17

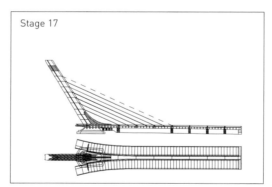

removal of temporary support between deck caissons 4 and 5
14-Aug-91 post-tension of cable stays no. 7
20-Aug-91 placement of concrete inside 11th caisson of pylon
21-Aug-91 assembly of 12th caisson of pylon
23-Aug-91 removal of scaffolding of concrete part of deck close to pedestal

Stage 18

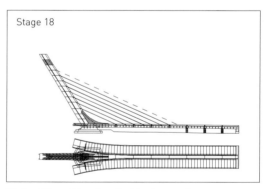

29-Aug-91 post-tension of cable stays no. 8
30-Aug-91 placement of concrete inside 12th caisson of pylon
03-Sep-91 assembly of 13th caisson of pylon

Stage 19

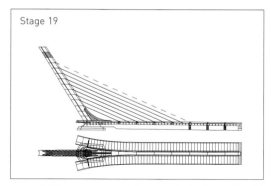

removal of temporary support between deck caissons 5 and 6
13-Sep-91 post-tension of cable stays no. 9
16-Sep-91 placement of concrete inside 13th caisson
of pylon
25-Sep-91 assembly of 14th caisson of pylon

Stage 20

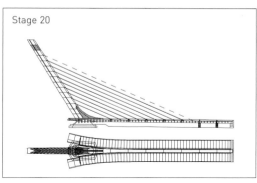

27-Sep-91 post-tension of cable stays no. 10
30-Sep-91 placement of concrete inside 14th caisson
of pylon
13-Oct-91 assembly of 15th caisson of pylon

Stage 21

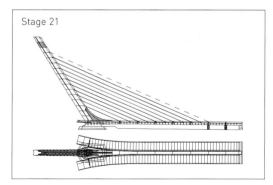

removal of temporary support between deck caissons 6 and 7
15-Oct-91 post-tension of cable stays no. 11
17-Oct-91 placement of concrete inside 15th caisson
of pylon
22-Oct-91 assembly of 16th caisson of pylon

Stage 22

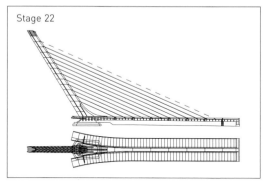

30-Oct-91 post-tension of cable stays no. 12
06-Nov-91 placement of concrete inside 16th caisson of
of pylon
09-Nov-91 removal of temporary support between deck
caissons 7 and 8

Stage 23

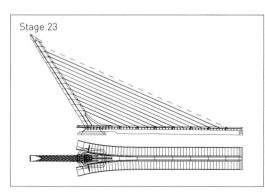

15-Nov-91 post-tension of cable stays no. 13
16-Nov-91 assembly of the head of the pylon

Stage 24

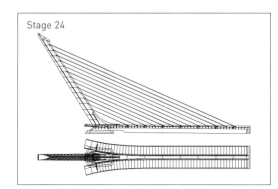

16-Nov-91 placement of concrete at base of head; finishes

Fig. 5.6 | The last 12 of the 24 stages of the construction of the bridge. Activities shown in gray on plan
and elevation.

5.4
CONTROL AND INSTRUMENTATION

The structural behavior of the bridge depends heavily on the weights of the deck and the pylon and on the tension of the cables (see section 4.2). Thus, precise information on those elements was necessary during construction in order to make corrections and reach the most desirable state of stresses. During construction, in addition to testing the properties of the structural materials, the following control points were established:

- control of the weights of the various elements of the deck and the pylon,
- topographical control of the exact alignment of the pylon,
- control of the reactions at the temporary supports of the deck,
- control of the tension of the cable stays at the pylon side,
- control of the stresses at the connection of the deck to the pedestal of the pylon,
- temperature control of the deck, the cable stays, and the pylon.

Vicrusa SA of Seville was contracted to design, install, and maintain a complete and per-

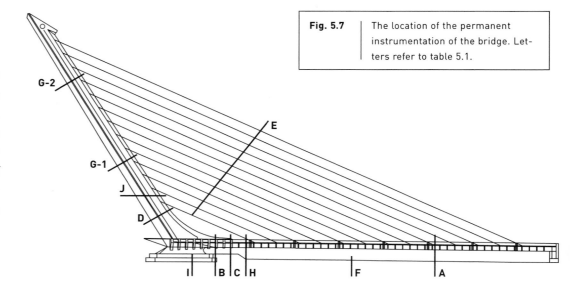

Fig. 5.7 | The location of the permanent instrumentation of the bridge. Letters refer to table 5.1.

manent instrumentation of the bridge. The permanent instrumentation served a triple purpose: first, it provided the necessary readings for certain critical operations on the bridge during construction, such as the tensioning of the cable stays, the construction of the deck, and the gradual removal of the temporary supports; second, it provided continuous feedback for verifying the structural calculations during construction; and third, it continues to give automatic readings of environmental loads and the corresponding structural response during the operation of the bridge, keeping updated rec-

ords of the bridge's behavior under normal and extreme loading conditions and of any permanent deformations of the bridge during its lifetime.

The 341 permanent instruments on the bridge (fig. 5.7 and table 5.1) provide information at the most critical sections of the corresponding structural elements on the following measurements:

- bending moments,
- axial and shearing stresses,

Reference	Section	Purpose	Instrumentation
A	Deck, axis 15	Bending moment Axial force Temperature expansion/contraction Thermal gradient	7 longitudinal bars for steel 6 concrete extensometers 6 steel thermometers 3 concrete thermometers
B	Deck, axis 47	Bending moment Axial force Concrete yielding Thermal gradient	8 steel extensometers 14 concrete extensometers 1 longitudinal bar for steel 11 concrete thermometers
C	Deck, boundary of steel and composite sections	Bending moment Axial force Temperature expansion/contraction Thermal gradient	6 longitudinal bars for steel 10 steel rosette bands 7 concrete extensometers 5 steel thermometers 3 concrete thermometers 1 steel extensometer
D	Pylon, base	Bending moment	24 longitudinal bars for steel 10 concrete extensometers 10 steel extensometers 6 steel thermometers 10 concrete thermometers
E	Cable stays	Axial force on cable stays	156 longitudinal bars for steel 2 pressure transductors 1 thermometer
F	Instrumented supports	Support reactions	8 temporary support devices
G-1	Pylon, caisson 7	Pylon inclination Thermal gradient	1 inclinometer 4 thermometers
G-2	Pylon, caisson 12	Pylon inclination Thermal gradient and concrete hardening	1 inclinometer 6 thermometers
H	Deck, axis 42	Stresses	1 steel extensometer 1 concrete extensometer
I	Foundations	Foundation rotation	1 inclinometer 1 thermometer
J	Pylon, level 40	Thermal gradient Concrete hardening temperature	10 concrete thermometers

Table 5.1 The permanent instrumentation of the bridge. See fig. 5.7 for locations.

- temperature variations across structural elements,
- hardening temperatures in concrete elements,
- tension forces in cable stays,
- inclination of the pylon,
- settlements and rotations of the foundation,
- reactions at supports,
- temperature and wind information.

Such extensive instrumentation is not common in bridges of this size—testimony to the precision required for the stability of the Alamillo Bridge.

5.5
STRUCTURAL ANALYSIS
DURING CONSTRUCTION

Computer-based structural analyses of the bridge were carried out to determine the stresses in the structural elements during each of the 42 construction steps shown in table 5.2. The model of the structural analysis of the bridge shown in fig. 4.1 was used as the basis for the structural analysis during construction. For practical reasons, the analysis of the 42 steps was carried out in reverse, starting from the complete model and removing the corresponding elements, weights, and tensioning forces.

A slightly different geometry for the finite element model was used in the analysis until construction step 27. Up to that point, the transition element between the deck and the pylon had not yet been built, so the three finite elements that modeled the lower part of the pylon were relocated to correspond to the orientation of the axis of the pylon without the transition element. The maximum translation occurred at the base of the pylon, where node 1 was moved horizontally 2.5 m away from the deck. The adjusted model more accurately predicted the behavior of the pylon during construction.

During the design phase, the results of the structural analyses were used to check the strength of the bridge's structural elements and redesign them accordingly. During construction, the analyses were repeated using the actual weights of the constructed elements. According to the records, the weight of the deck exceeded the design estimates by 4%, and the weight of the pylon exceeded them by 2%. The temperature was set at both the minimum and the maximum design values for the structural analysis at each construction step, taking into account adjusted tensioning forces of the cable stays for each temperature setting. The data were based on the detailed records that had been kept during tensioning, including the tensioning force and the temperature.

The results of the structural analyses were compared to the actual readings from the sensors on the bridge in order to ensure a construction process as planned. The early comparisons between structural analyses and the actual data obtained from the bridge's instrumentation showed that the pylon deflected more than had been predicted. Reduced stiffness in the pylon was caused by hairline cracking in the concrete as a result of high temperatures during hardening, and by an actual modulus of elasticity of concrete that was smaller than the one that had been used in the calculations (reduced from 34,825 MPa to 29,430 MPa).[1] After this reduction, the calculated deflections were compatible with the measured deflections and the analytical model was used reliably to predict the remaining construction steps.

1   The structural analysis in chapter 4 was based on the updated weights of the structural elements and the reduced modulus of elasticity of concrete.

Table 5.2 The 42 different steps of the construction of the bridge that were analyzed using finite elements.

1	Positioning of the segments of the steel box on the seven temporary supports
2	Welding of the segments of the steel box
3	Construction of the deck, including concrete, so it reaches the design load of 302.93 kN/m
4	Installation and placement of concrete in caissons 1, 2, 3, and 4 of the pylon, as well as at the reinforced concrete connection between the steel box of the deck and the pedestal
5	Positioning of the 5th caisson of the pylon
6	Tensioning of the 1st pair of cable stays
7	Placing concrete in the 5th caisson of the pylon
8–37	Steps 5, 6, and 7 for caissons of 6–15 and cable stays 2–11
38	Tensioning of the 12th pair of cable stays
39	Placement of concrete in the 16th caisson of the pylon, and positioning of the head of the pylon
40	Tensioning of the 13th pair of cable stays
41	Removal of the temporary supports of the deck
42	Placing the asphalt on the roadways

6 CONSTRUCTION

Of Calatrava's initial proposal for the two bridges and viaduct of the Paso del Alamillo, only the cable-stayed bridge on the Seville side and the viaduct of the Cartuja were built according to his designs (fig. 6.1). The temporary association of companies (UTE) "Puente de Alamillo" of Dragados y Construcciones SA and Fomento de Construcciones y Contratas SA was awarded the construction and built the bridge.

The bid was based on partially completed sets of drawings that required further development. However, the contractors were very supportive of the design concept and sought more than just another job and profits. Pleased to participate in the construction of such an important engineering project, certain to receive national and international recognition, they did not argue against innovations or claim inexperience with similar structures. Neither did they ask for unreasonable compensation for the many change orders. Above all, the contractors were willing to assume risks and responsibilities beyond contractual obligations in order to see the bridge built as close to Calatrava's intentions as possible.

The Alamillo Bridge was constructed in 31 months, following the construction schedule

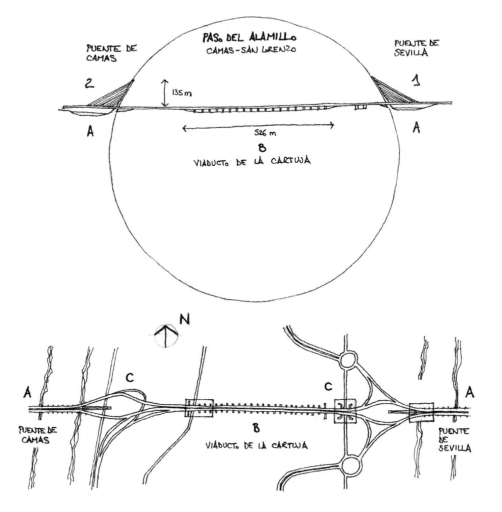

Fig. 6.1 Plan and elevation of the Paso del Alamillo Camas-San Lázaro master plan as envisioned by Calatrava. The project included two 140-m-high asymmetrical cable-stayed bridges (A), a 526-m-long multiple-span viaduct (B), and two circulation nodes (C). The Seville bridge (1) was to cross the old course of the river between Cartuja Island (site of Expo '92) and Seville's neighborhood of San Lázaro. The Camas bridge (2) was to cross the present course of the river between Cartuja Island and the small town of Camas. The viaduct and the Seville bridge (the Alamillo Bridge) were eventually built following Calatrava's design. For economic as well as political reasons, the Camas bridge was built as a conventional structure.

described in chapter 5. On February 29, 1992, the bridge was load-tested, just 42 days before the opening of Expo '92. The official opening of the bridge was delayed until March 12, 1992, waiting for MOPU's Cartuja-Camas bridge on the other side of the island to be completed. The Alamillo Bridge has been in operation continuously since that day.

The cost of the bridge exceeded the initial budget. The actual cost was 3,850 million pesetas ($38.5 million; see appendix B). Such an amount corresponds to approximately 547,000 pesetas ($5,470) per square meter of horizontal surface. Cost increases were attributed to the unconventional construction, which required elaborate studies and reduced productivity. The quantities of concrete and steel used are also high compared to those of bridges of a comparable span. The contractors made an effort to reduce the total cost of the bridge by simplifying both the construction process and many details, and by standardizing the elements as much as possible without changing the spirit of the design.

Fig. 6.2 shows the main dimensions of the bridge. Six construction entities compose the entire bridge. They are presented here in the order of the construction process: foundations, pedestal of the pylon, deck, pylon, cable stays, and finishes.

6.1
FOUNDATIONS

The bridge is supported on two foundations: that of the pylon, which takes most of the loads, and that of the east abutment.

The foundation of the pylon (fig. 6.3) is designed to withstand forces and moments in all directions with minimum tolerances for deformations and rotations. Fifty-four reinforced concrete piles embedded in the marl constitute the foundation of the pylon. Each pile has a diameter of 2 m and a free length of 45.5 m. The distance from pile to pile is approximately 3.25 m center to center and they are all connected to a 4.5 m deep pile cap. The reinforced concrete pile cap was placed in two steps.

For each pile, segments of steel tube were driven by a hydraulic hammer until they reached the marl. The enclosed sand and gravel was then removed using a clamshell excavator. After each steel tube was emptied, the marl was drilled 24 m further. Next, the spiral reinforcing steel was positioned inside the hole by crane. The spiral reinforcement included 36 longitudinal 25 mm bars distributed at the perimeter of the pile. Finally, concrete was placed and the steel tube of the upper part of the pile was extracted using vibration.

The east abutment was designed to support the vertical and horizontal loads and torsional moments of the steel box of the deck. The hexagonal steel box enters 2.20 m into the reinforced concrete abutment, where it is supported by a heavy steel beam on top of a post-tensioned concrete beam (see fig. 6.15). Neoprene cushions allow the deck to expand or contract The hexagonal shape of the box entering the hexagonal opening provides the torsional support for the deck. Simple bearing supports the steel box laterally.

Fig. 6.2	Elevation of the Alamillo Bridge showing the main dimensions of the pylon, the pedestal, and the deck. The pylon consists of 17 caissons, including the head caisson. The deck is divided into eight segments, approximately 24 m long. The highest point of the pylon (D) is 141.25 m above water level. The total span of the bridge is 219 m. The span of the deck between the axis of the pylon (C) and that of the east abutment (A) is 200 m. The deck of the bridge slopes down 1% toward the east: the roadway at the pedestal of the pylon (B) is 2.35 m higher than the roadway at the east abutment (A).

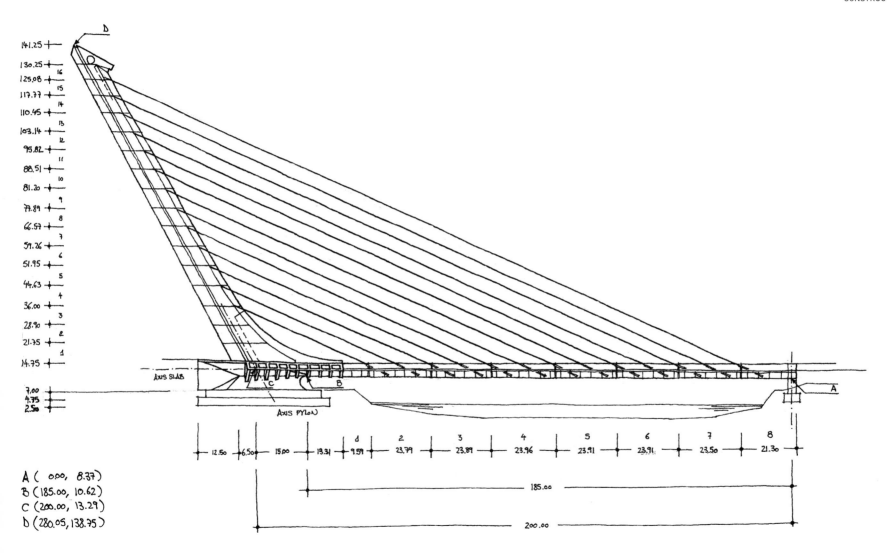

141.25
130.25
125.08   16
117.77   15
110.45   14
103.14   13
95.82   12
88.51   11
81.20   10
77.89   9
66.57   8
59.26   7
51.95   6
44.63   5
36.00   4
28.90   3
21.75   2
14.75   1

7.00
4.75
2.50

AXIS SLAB

AXIS PYLON

A (0.00, 8.37)
B (185.00, 10.62)
C (200.00, 13.29)
D (280.05, 138.75)

12.50 6.50 15.00 13.31 9.59 23.79 23.89 23.96 23.91 23.91 23.50 21.30

1   2   3   4   5   6   7   8

185.00

200.00

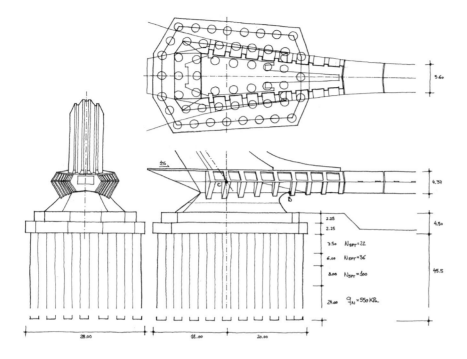

Fig. 6.3	Drawings of the foundation showing the 2-m-diameter piles, the octagonal pile cap, and the pedestal. The pylon is supported by 54 reinforced concrete piles embedded in the marl. The center of the foundation is vertically aligned with the intersection of the axis of the pylon and the deck (C). Information on the soil profile is given next to the piles.

Access to the interior of the main steel box is provided through a hexagonal gate on the face of the vertical wall of the east abutment. The gate is positioned exactly below the steel box, its shape identical to the cross section of the box but smaller. The use of the same shape provides a visual relationship between the entry and the interior of the box.

6.2
PEDESTAL

The pedestal, constructed on top of the pile cap (fig. 6.4), provides the transition between the pylon's foundation and the level of the deck. Made of exposed white reinforced concrete, the lower part of the pedestal has inclined flat surfaces. At the

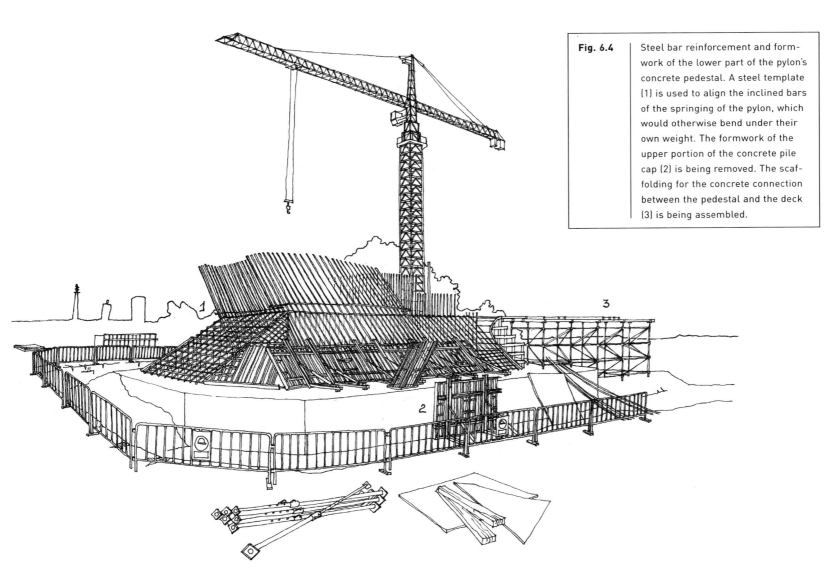

Fig. 6.4 | Steel bar reinforcement and formwork of the lower part of the pylon's concrete pedestal. A steel template (1) is used to align the inclined bars of the springing of the pylon, which would otherwise bend under their own weight. The formwork of the upper portion of the concrete pile cap (2) is being removed. The scaffolding for the concrete connection between the pedestal and the deck (3) is being assembled.

Fig. 6.5 | Completion of the pylon's pedestal. The pylon's lowest steel caisson (1) has already been aligned and embedded in the pedestal's concrete core. The scaffolding at the back of the pedestal (2) will support the connection with the west abutment. On the opposite side, the reinforcement and formwork of the concrete part of the deck are being assembled (3). Concrete and steel elements will support the cantilevering roadways along the pedestal (4).

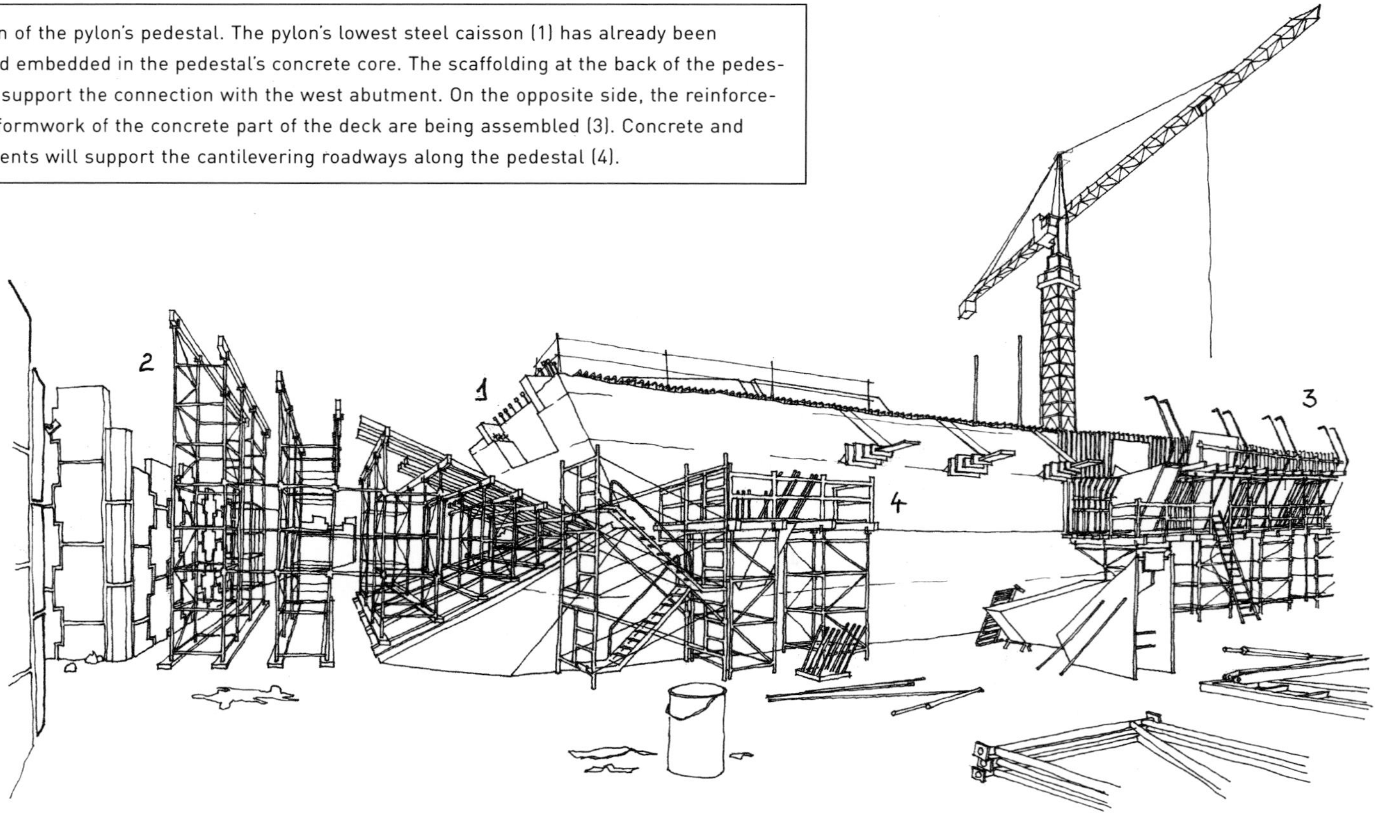

back of the pylon, the slope is 30° to the horizontal, and at the two sides it is 52°. On the upper part of the pedestal, these inclinations are reversed (fig. 6.5). On the east (front) side, the connection between the pedestal and the lower part of the steel deck is curved, following a cylindrical surface; above this, the shape of the pedestal starts initially follows the shape of the steel box and gradually converges to assume the curves of the pylon.

Steel anchors embedded in the reinforced concrete provide the tension support of the cantilevering wings of the roadway at the base of the pylon (fig. 6.6). Reinforced concrete elements below each anchor provide the compression supports for the

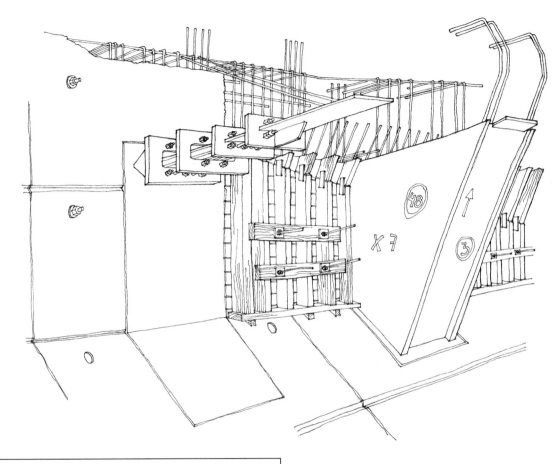

Fig. 6.6   A detail of one of the pedestal's walls during construction. The view shows reinforcing steel bars, formwork, and two of the brackets, or "ribs," that will support the cantilevered wings of the roadway. The rib in the foreground, at an early stage of construction, reveals its interior steel plate and threaded rod anchoring system. Later, it will be enclosed in a steel formwork (such as the one marked "48") and will be filled with concrete.

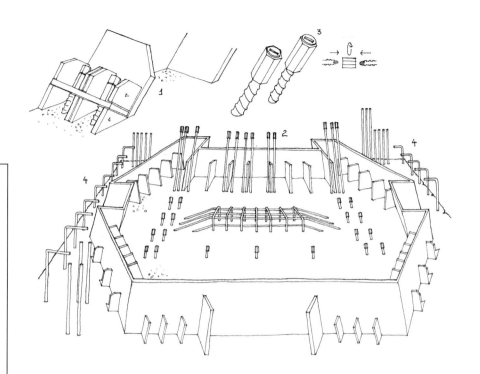

Fig. 6.7 A view of the lowest steel caisson (number 0) from the deck looking west. This is the section of the bridge where high stresses will develop, and from which the pylon will spring. There are hundreds of reinforcement bars (only some are shown), and construction quality control was intense. The steel caisson and the reinforcement bars were precisely aligned, and the quality of concrete and steel was thoroughly tested. Steel plates and bars served as anchors for the connection of the pedestal and the caisson (1). Some steel bars extended to higher levels (2). The high-strength steel bars could not be welded, and threaded nuts provided the connection. Plastic caps (3) protected the threaded part of the bars during placement of concrete. The reinforcement bars outside the caisson (4) are part of the pedestrian walkway around the pylon.

wings. Eight of these steel wings spring from each side of the pedestal, at 4 m intervals. Skylights are located in the space between the supports of the steel wings and next to the pedestal to admit natural light under the bridge.

The lowest steel caisson of the pylon (caisson 0) was placed on top of the pedestal to start the construction of the pylon. It was embedded in the reinforced concrete to ensure a structural continuity, with only 1.60 m extruded (fig. 6.7). The pedestrian walkway was constructed adjacent to the base of the pylon on both sides.

The upper part of the pedestal extends 23 m eastbound toward the deck from the center point between the pylon and the pedestal (point C in fig. 6.2). At that point, the pedestal ends and the steel

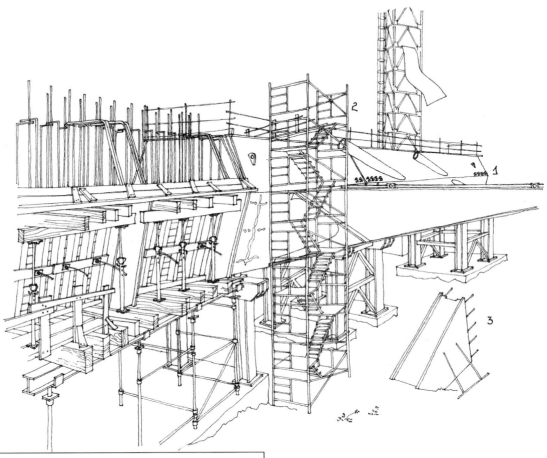

Fig. 6.8 | Scaffolding and formwork of the pedestal-deck connection. The drawing shows the segment of the deck that connects the pylon's concrete pedestal (enclosed in formwork, to the left) and the temporarily supported steel box (1). A temporary stairway provides access to the top of the steel box (2). One of the steel caissons for making the ribs supporting the roadways along the pedestal awaits placement (3).

box that supports the main deck of the bridge begins (fig. 6.8; see fig. 6.18 for details of the transition).

The construction of the upper part of the pedestal took a long time to finish because it required extensive in situ work on the formwork and the reinforcement. While the construction of the pedestal continued, work on the pylon and the main deck proceeded.

6.3
THE DECK

The deck is composed of a hexagonal steel box running along the longitudinal axis of the bridge, pairs of cantilevering steel wings that support the cantilevering roadway on both sides of the hexagonal box, and the concrete slabs that form the roadway. The cable stays support the hexagonal box every 12 m, while the steel wings are positioned every 4 m.

Fig. 6.9 shows half the cross section of the deck of the bridge and its dimensions. Each roadway has 3 lanes of traffic. The main pedestrian walkway is 3.75 m wide, located on the top of the hexagonal box at the center of the deck and elevated 1.80 m above the roadway. Emergency narrow walkways are provided at both edges of the deck.

The geometry of the deck changes as it approaches the pylon. The steel box first widens and is partially filled with reinforced concrete. Then it becomes a concrete element, constituting the upper part of the pedestal for the pylon. At that section of the bridge the roadways curve, but they still cantilever from the pedestal. Two post-tensioned concrete slabs make up the last part of the deck between the pedestal and the west abutment, extending over a road perpendicular to the axis of the bridge.

6.3.1
TEMPORARY SUPPORTS

The uncoupling of the construction of the deck and the pylon, for the sake of construction efficiency, required the temporary support of the deck on the shallow riverbed, where an earth embankment was constructed to provide the necessary working space (fig. 6.10). Large pipes were placed across the embankment to maintain the flow of the Meandro de San Jerónimo. Seven temporary supports were installed along the embankment to hold the entire deck during its construction, until the pylon was ready and the cable stays could transfer the weight of the deck to the pylon. The temporary steel supports were space frames, with each support providing four vertical columns. Neoprene and neoprene Teflon were used on top of the columns to provide a smooth support for the steel box and allow horizontal movement. Because of the heavy load of the deck and the minimum tolerances for settlement, the temporary supports had their own deep foundations, consisting of reinforced concrete piers embedded in the upper sand layers (see fig. 4.15 for the soil profile). Concrete piers were constructed underneath the riverbed; the steel space frame started at the level of the riverbed and continued through the earth embankment to the required level to support the deck. Disassembling these temporary structures was quite easy after the construction was completed, and no demolition of concrete was necessary.

6.3.2
THE STEEL BOX

The hexagonal steel box along the longitudinal axis of the deck provides the main structural support for the deck. The box has the necessary strength and stiffness for the vertical, horizontal, and torsional loads that act on the bridge's deck. It also provides a firm anchoring for the cable stays and supports the cantilevering roadways, though for architectural reasons it maintains a physical separa-

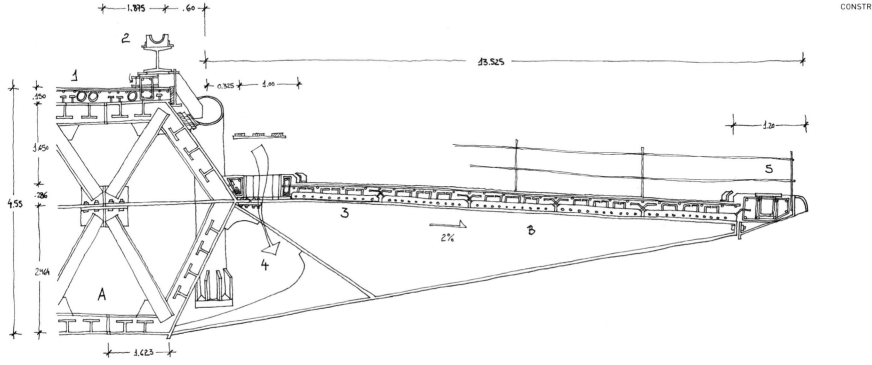

Fig. 6.9 The cross section of the steel box and the cantilevering roadway during construction. A site-cast concrete slab poured on the steel box (A) forms the bridge's pedestrian walkway (1). Tracks for the assembly and sliding of the cable stays are built on the precast concrete edge of the walkway (2). Prefabricated concrete slabs spanning between the steel wings (3) serve as formwork for the site-cast concrete of the roadways (B). Natural light reaches under the deck through openings in the inner curb of the slab (4). The roadway slab slopes outward 2% and drains through openings next to the outer curb. Steel plates embedded in both the inner and outer curbs (5) serve as anchors for the roadway's guard rails.

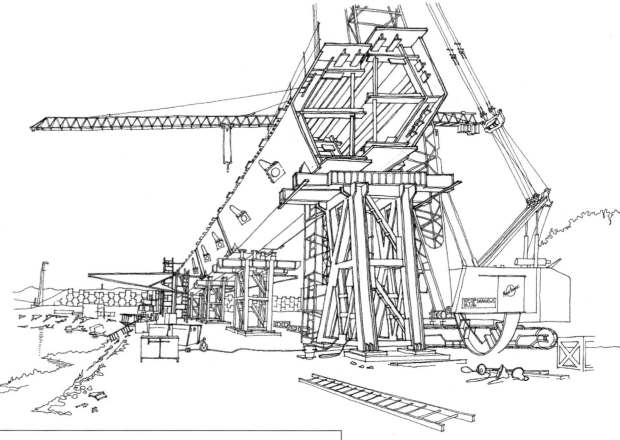

Fig. 6.10 | Positioning of one of the segments of the deck's steel box. The course of the river has been filled and temporary structures built to support the deck. The left and right pieces of each of the 24-m-long segments of the steel box were transported separately and welded at their final location. The pass-through tubes for the cable stays and anchor plates for the roadway's canti-levering wings were prefabricated on the box. Here, the first wings, close to the pylon, are being positioned, as seen in the background.

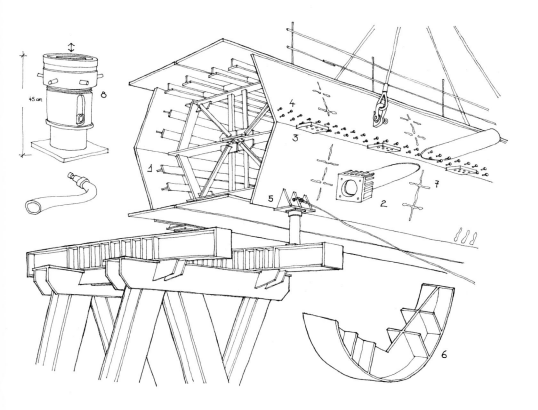

Fig. 6.11 | A detail of the deck's steel box during assembly. Both the left and the right pieces that compose each segment of the box are made of four plates, incorporating internal stiffeners (1), pass-through tubes for the cable stays (2), anchor plates for the cantilevering wings (3), shear connectors for the roadway's concrete slab (4), and brackets for temporary support (5). Temporary steel elements, called "skates" (6), simplified the lifting operation by allowing free rotation of each piece during lifting. Once the piece was rotated and lifted, the skates were removed, leaving characteristic marks (7). Hydraulic jacks were used for precise alignment (8).

tion from the roadways. Its weight is compatible with the overall equilibrium of the bridge.

The depth of the box is constant along its entire length at 4.40 m. The top and the bottom of the box are variable in width. For a distance of 136 m from the east abutment, the top is 3.75 m wide and the bottom is 3.246 m wide. Then the box widens, with its sides following an elliptical curve; at its west end, 171.5 m from the east abutment, it reaches 6.394 m wide at the top and 5.89 m at the bottom.

The steel box is made from sheet plates 50 mm thick. The top plate of the box overhangs the inclined side plate by 60 mm, while the lower inclined plates extend the same distance beyond the bottom plate, to allow water to drip (fig. 6.11). Eighteen T-section beams along the longitudinal axis, inside the box, provide additional stiffness for the plates. Four of those beams are welded to the top plate and four to the bottom plate of the box, two beams to each upper inclined plate, and three beams to each lower inclined plate of the box. Stiffening diaphragms are positioned every 4 m inside the box, at the points where the cable stays anchor and at the location of the cantilevering wings. These stiffening diaphragms consist of T-section beams welded perpendicular to the axis of the box, forming a closed hexagon; a strut that connects the two side edges inside the box and provides continuity for the cantilevering wings on the opposite sides of the box; and four angles that connect the four edges of the upper and lower plates with the center of the box.

The direct support of the box on the embankment and the separate construction of the deck and the pylon allowed the building of the steel box in eight segments. Six of those segments were approximately 24 m each; the first segment close to the pylon was 9.59 m, and the last segment close to the east abutment was 21.30 m (see fig. 6.2). The total length of the continuous steel box is 173.30 m, with 171.50 m being exposed and 2.20 m inside the east abutment. Each segment was prefabricated in two pieces, left and right (see fig. 6.10), with all the necessary attachments, including temporary supports for lifting by the crane and for positioning on the temporary scaffolding (see fig. 6.11). The pass-through tubes for the cable stays were welded through the box, at a 24° angle

with the horizontal. Steel plates were attached to the box to connect the cantilevering wings. Shear connectors along the box were installed to provide a monolithic connection between the roadway slabs and the box, to ensure diaphragmatic action for horizontal loads. The dimensioning of the box and the spacing and size of the cantilevering wings were determined by space requirements for the hydraulic jacks used for the post-tensioning of the cable stays.

The pieces of the steel box were transported to the site by ground transportation. They were positioned on the temporary supports on the earth embankment by a Manitowoc 4100 crane (fig. 6.12). The crane had a boom of 33 m and a radius of 8 m for a maximum weight of 1,100 kN. Each segment of the box was supported on scaffolding on the riverbed at four points. Hydraulic jacks were employed to ensure proper alignment, prior to the final welding (fig. 6.13). That alignment included a calculated camber along the axis of the bridge in order to achieve the final alignment of the deck after the completion of the construction when it would be subject to the full dead loads.

The lower part of the steel box was filled with reinforced concrete for the 36 m nearest to the pedestal. The reinforced concrete almost entirely fills the steel box interior for the first 11 m where no

cable stays are attached, leaving only an inspection opening 4.40 m wide and 1.80 m high, located near the center axis of the box. The cross-sectional area of the concrete in that part reaches 23.5 m^2. Then it tapers for the next 25 m. The added concrete provides a smoother transition of the forces from the steel box to the concrete pedestal, to increase the compression strength. It also adds weight to the deck for equilibrium in the segment that is supported by the first three pairs of cable stays.

| Fig. 6.12 | The Manitowoc 4100 crane positions a piece of the deck's steel box. The previous segment (1) is already positioned on fixed neoprene supports, while the new one is being leveled with hydraulic jacks. The space between the two segments (2) is an access opening and will be closed later. |

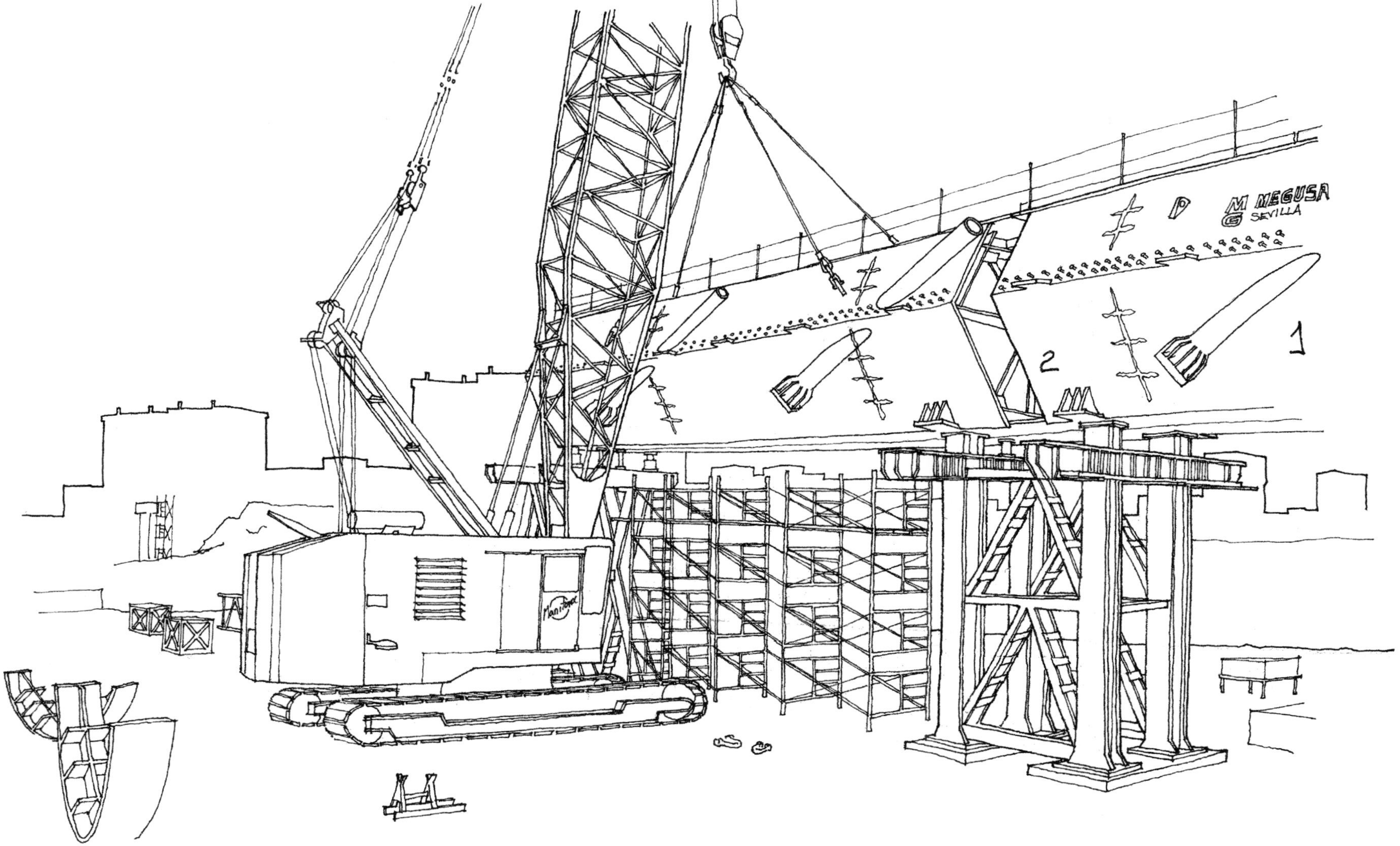
MEGUSA
SEVILLA
2
1

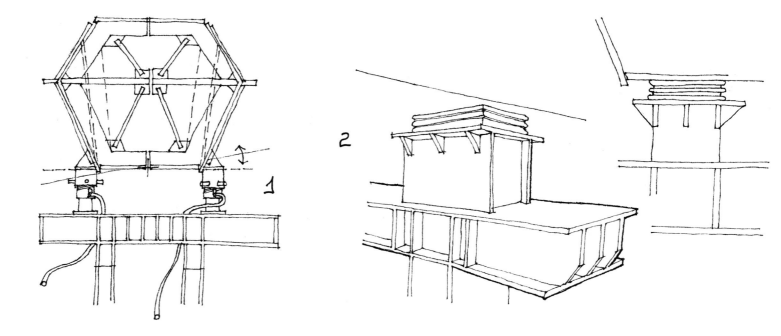

Fig. 6.13 | Details of the deck's steel box and the connections of the roadway's wings. The box is leveled with hydraulic jacks (1), then supported on neoprene cushions (2) during the rest of the construction process. The neoprene supports allow a longitudinal movement of the deck. The connection of the cantilevering wings to the steel box (see drawing at top right) consists of a tension connection (3) at the side edge of the hexagon and a compression connection (4) at the lowest part of the box. The loads are transferred to the box as shown on the schematic diagram (5). The tension connection is bolted, with high-strength shearing bolts (6). The compression connection is simply welded. Adjacent parts of wings are connected at their free edge by a steel bracket (7). That element is part of the formwork for the concrete roadway.

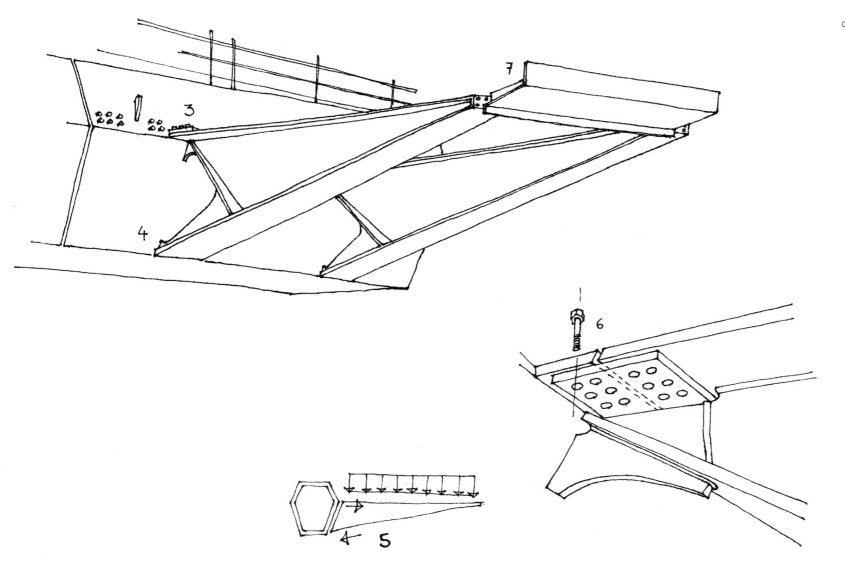

6.3.3
CANTILEVERING STEEL WINGS

Forty-three pairs of identical wings are attached along the steel box. Each 12 m long steel wing weighs 58 kN and is connected to the box at two points only, a tensile connection at the top and a compressive connection at the bottom. These connections are quite expressive and were engineered according to Calatrava's extensive studies of tension and compression and his experiments in sculpture. Each wing depicts the flow of forces and the transformation of the moment connection of the cantilever to the tension on the top and the compression on the bottom. The shearing forces are transferred by an additional piece, attached to the tensile connection, perpendicular to the top flange of the wing. This piece was welded onto the steel box after the bolts had been tightened.

The cantilevering steel wings were prefabricated, transported to the site, and positioned using the same crane that positioned the steel box segments. Their exact positioning was controlled topographically, similarly to determining the positions of the steel box and the pylon, and was facilitated by reflectors located on their free edge. Once positioned, the top flange of the wing was aligned with the welded plate and an auxiliary plate was bolted

with 24 high-strength bolts to make a shearing tensile connection. The connection in compression was welded in situ on the lower part of the box. Steel brackets then connected the outside edges of the steel wings, providing the outer piece of the formwork for the roadways and defining the edge of the bridge.

6.3.4
ROADWAY SLABS

The wings support the slabs that form the roadway of the bridge without any girders. The one-way continuous slabs have a free span of 4 m between consecutive wings. The composite slab was made with prefabricated concrete elements below and a cast-on-site slab on the top (fig. 6.14).

Eighty different types of the prefabricated elements were made, all 100 mm thick, reinforced with longitudinal steel, and with shear connectors rising from their tops. The prefabricated elements were transported by the same crane as the steel box segments and the cantilevering wings, and were positioned on the top flanges of sequential steel wings. A 130 mm thick concrete slab, containing additional reinforcing steel along both longitudinal and transverse axes, was then cast on top, integrating with the lower precast pieces to form a single

Fig. 6.14 | Construction of the pedestrian walkway and roadway slabs: shear connectors on the prefabricated concrete slabs (1) and the steel box (2); skylights (3); steel edge elements (4); steel plates for the anchoring of guard rails (5); and steel curb formwork pieces (6). The precast concrete edge elements for the pedestrian walkway (7) are interrupted by their intersection with the cables. The first three caissons of the pylon and the two fixed cranes used for the construction of the bridge are shown in the background.

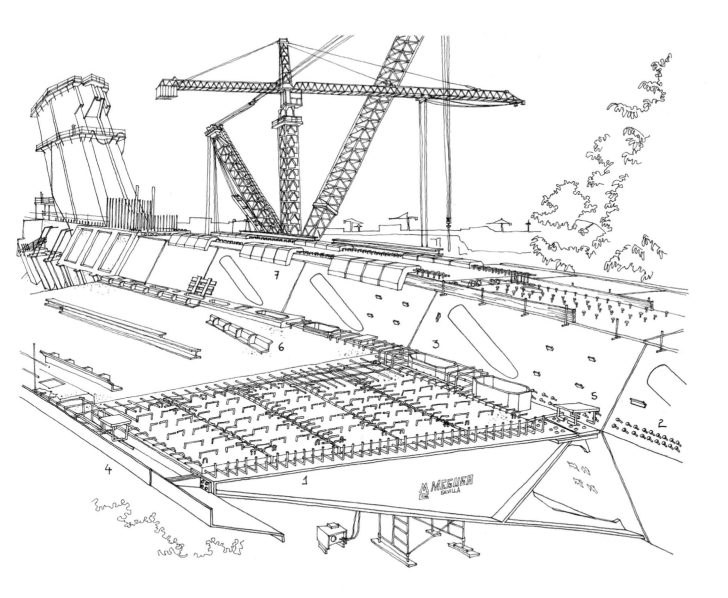

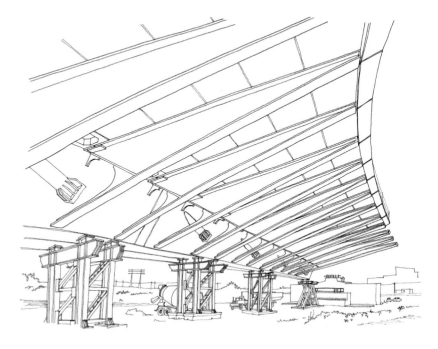

structural slab. This construction process eliminated the use of temporary formwork and ensured a high quality of the exposed concrete under the bridge (fig. 6.15).

The slab for the roadway extends laterally all the way to the steel box, where shear connectors ensure continuity between the slab and the steel box. Two skylights were placed between consecutive steel wings to allow natural light to reach under the bridge and to establish a visual break between the box and the roadways (figs. 6.14, 6.15). Such an effort reflected Calatrava's original proposal of a complete separation between the steel box and the roadways.

The construction of the pedestal of the pylon continued during the construction of the main deck of the bridge and of the pylon (figs. 6.16, 6.17). Along the pedestal, the structure of the roadway remains the same as in the main deck, although it

Fig. 6.15 | A view under the deck, looking east toward the San Lázaro neighborhood of Seville. The east abutment is under construction, and the last segment of the steel box has not been positioned yet.

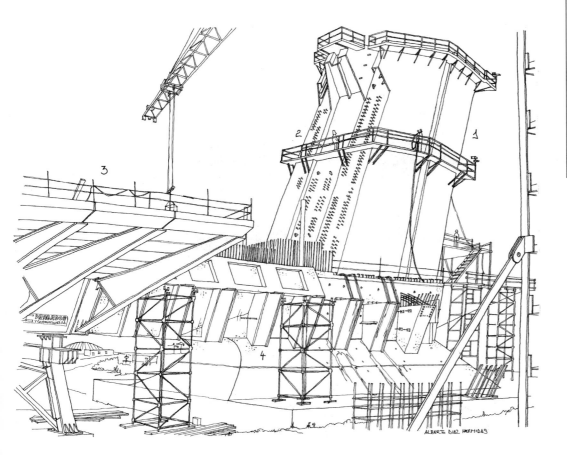

ALBERTO DIAZ HERMIDAS

Fig. 6.16 | A view of the pedestal, the deck, and the pylon. The third steel caisson (1) is being secured in place from a temporary welding platform. Shear connectors on the second and third caissons (2) will ensure their bonding with the reinforced concrete of the curving transition element between the pylon and the deck. One of the roadways is being assembled (3); the drawing shows its cantilevering steel wings and pre-fabricated concrete slabs spanning between the wings. Brackets for the positioning of additional steel wings are embedded in the concrete core of the pedestal (4).

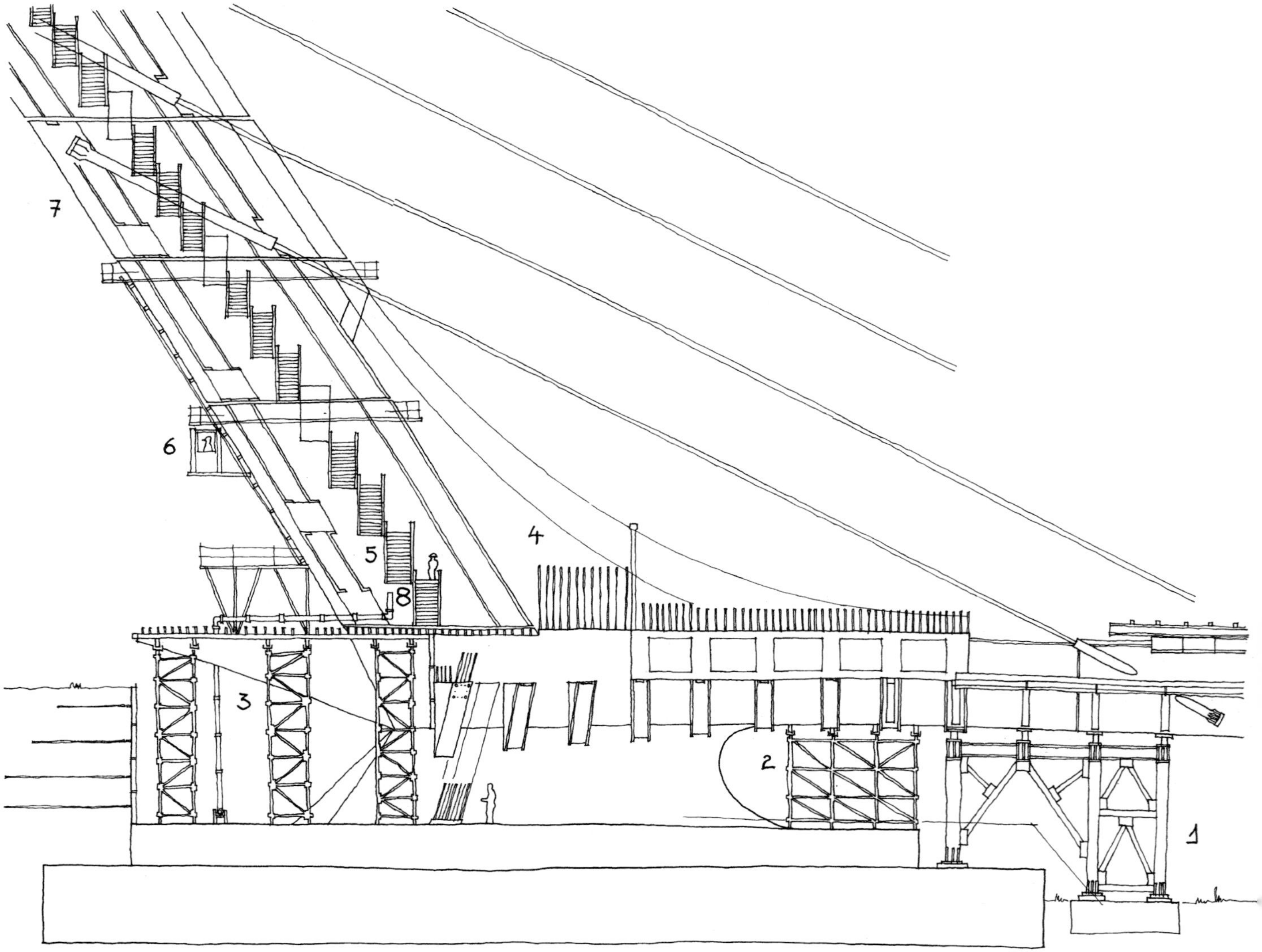
7
6
5
8
4
3
2
1

Fig. 6.17 | Schematic cross section of the pile cap and the pedestal. The first of the temporary steel structures supporting the steel deck is shown to the right (1). A lighter scaffolding supports the concrete section connecting the steel deck and the pedestal (2). A large cantilevered element (3) spans between the pedestal and the abutment, while the moment connection between the pedestal and the pylon is reinforced by a curving concrete section (4). Access to the pylon is provided by an interior stairway (5) as well as a temporary exterior elevator (6). The first pair of cables is anchored to the fourth caisson (7) of the pylon. The concrete pumping pipe runs along the interior stairway well (8).

curves to embrace the base of the pylon (fig. 6.18). Eight pairs of steel wings cantilever from the pedestal to support the roadway, as discussed in section 6.2.

6.3.5
DECK IN BACK OF THE PYLON

In back of the pylon, next to the west abutment, a transverse road at the river bank level passes under the bridge. Two post-tensioned concrete slabs span that 16 m gap on either side of the pylon (fig. 6.19). On the bridge side, the slabs are supported on a Y-shaped reinforced concrete element (reminiscent of Calatrava's earlier forms, especially the steel columns of the Stadelhofen train station in Zurich and the concrete elements of the Satolas train station in Lyons). That element is aligned with the steel wings but it is supported directly on the ground. On the other side, the slabs are supported on the abutment. The walls of the west abutment are covered by prefabricated concrete panels, the front end of an earth-retaining reinforcement that was quite common in Spain at that time. These cover plates were designed locally only after the bridge was under construction and are visually incompatible with it.

During construction, the post-tensioned slabs were supported on their own formwork of plywood on scaffolding, the only part of the roadway for which formwork and scaffolding were used (fig. 6.20). Supports of neoprene were installed at both ends of the slabs to allow expansion. The width of each slab is 13 m and their thickness is variable, ranging from 430 mm at the exterior edge to a maximum of 870 mm toward the pylon's side.

Eighteen tendons were used for post-tensioning a 5 m zone along the middle of the slab. Each tendon was made of nine 0.60 inch (15.24 mm) strands with a total area of 1,254 mm². The railings, light fixtures, and traffic barriers are the same over the post-tensioned concrete slabs (fig. 6.21) as they are along the rest of the bridge.

The pedestrian walkway does not follow the roadways in back of the pylon. Beyond the end of the steel box, the walkway continues on the pedestal and then divides in two, following each side of the pylon. The two branches merge again behind the pylon (see fig. 6.19), and the walkway crosses the transverse road under the bridge as a solid concrete cantilever from the back of the pedestal (fig. 6.23). Two stairways lead from the west abutment to the river bank, shown in fig. 6.19.

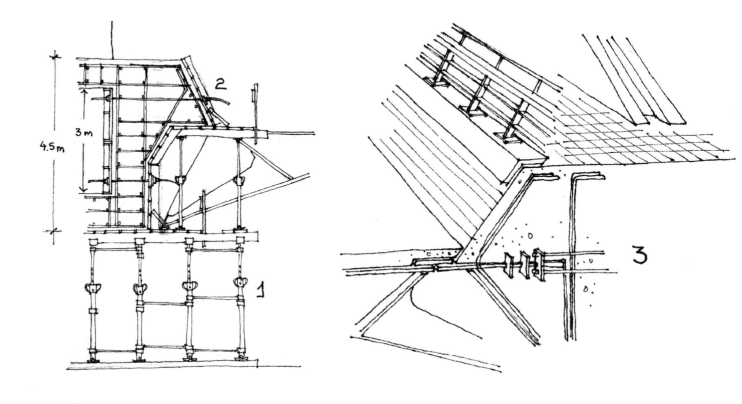

Fig. 6.18 | Various cross sections of the pedestal-deck connection. The formwork is supported by a scaffolding of telescopic steel supports and beams (1). Pass-through steel rods (2) prevent the horizontal deformation of the formwork. A steel plate anchored to the concrete core supports the steel wings of the roadways (3). A service gallery (4) allows access to the interior of the pedestal and the steel box for future inspections. The first part of the deck's steel box is partially filled with concrete (5) to increase its compression strength.

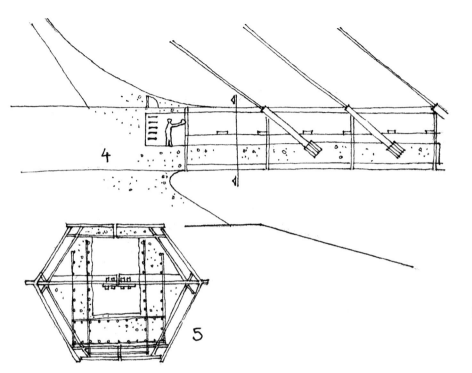

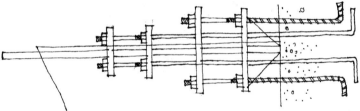

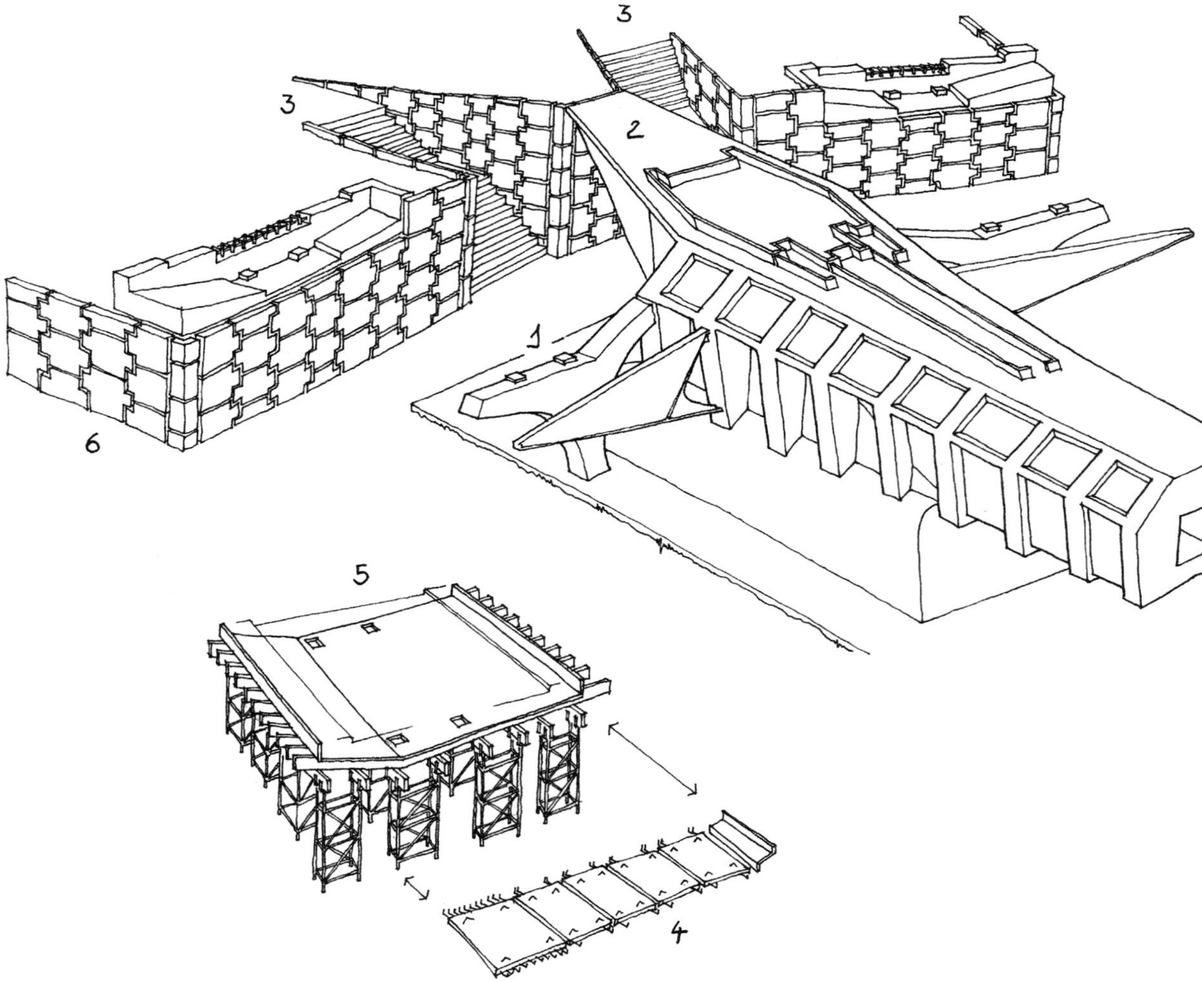
3
3
2
1
6
5
4

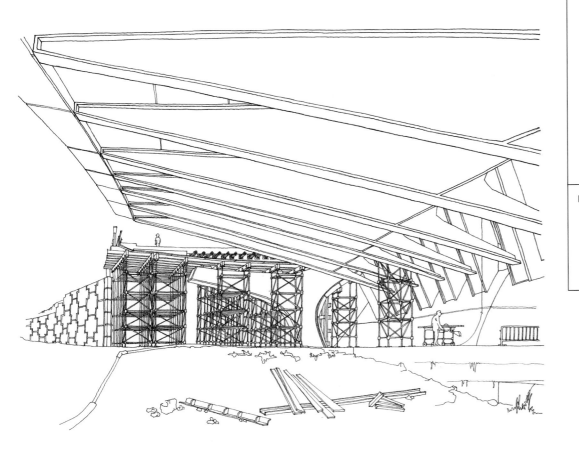

Fig. 6.19 | Schematic diagram of the bridge's pedestal and west abutments. Two 16-m-long post-tensioned concrete slabs span the gap. Each slab is supported on a Y-shaped reinforced concrete element (1). The pedestrian walkway cantilevers from the pedestal toward the central abutment (2). Two stairways separate the center and side abutments (3). Unlike the cantilevering roadways that used pre-cast concrete elements (4), the two post-tensioned slabs were cast in place over plywood formwork (5). The earth-retaining concrete panels were designed later, independently of the bridge (6).

Fig. 6.20 | One of the post-tensioned slabs viewed from under the roadway. The drawing shows the slab's post-tensioning wedges as well as the formwork for the slab and its Y-shaped concrete support.

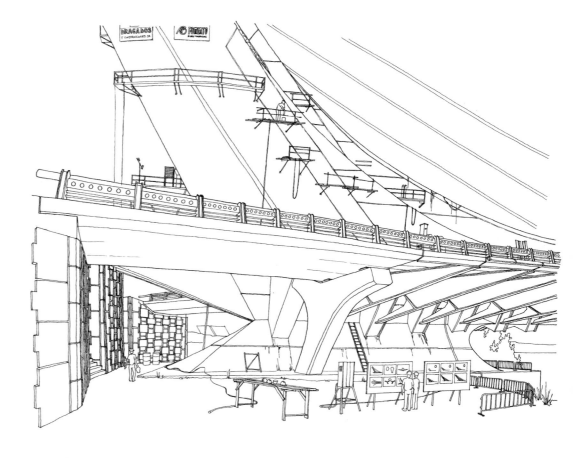

Fig. 6.21 | A view from the site's access road showing the abutments, the post-tensioned slabs, and the curved pylon-deck connection. The scaffolding of the post-tensioned slabs has been removed. Two visitors view drawings explaining the construction process. The logos of the two contractors are posted on the pylon. Note the size of the Y-shaped concrete element supporting the post-tensioned slab.

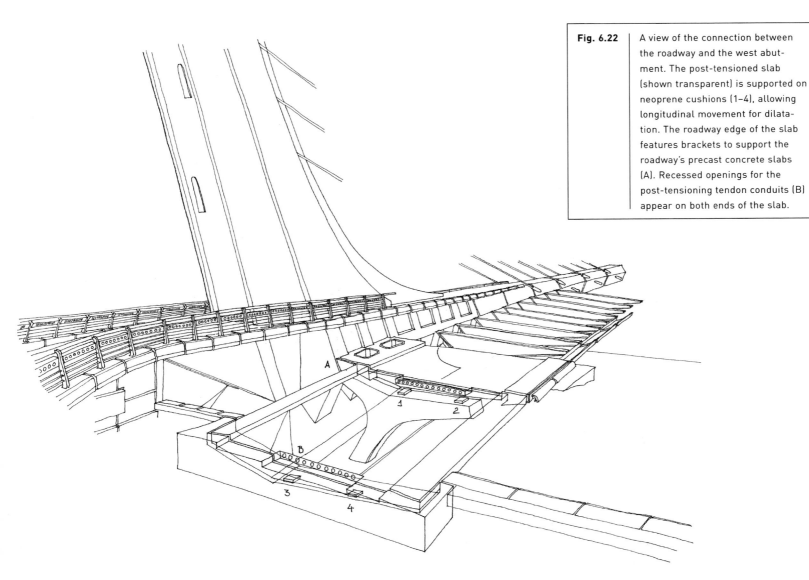

Fig. 6.23 | A view of the back of the pedestal from the west abutment looking south. The diagram shows the cantilevered pedestrian walkway and the Y-shaped reinforced concrete support for the post-tensioned slab of the roadway.

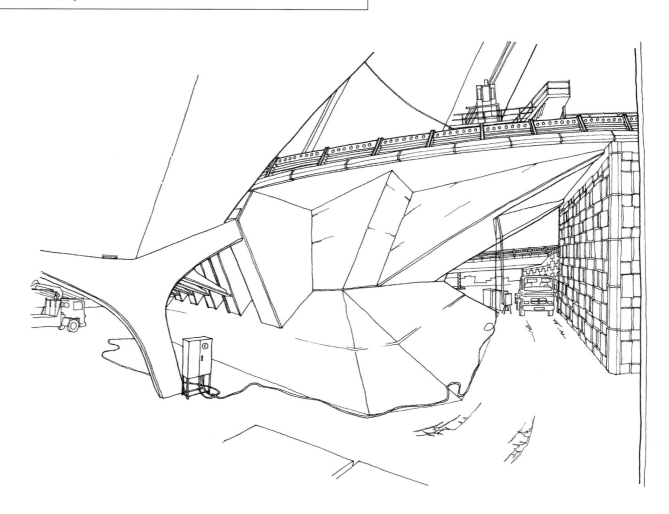

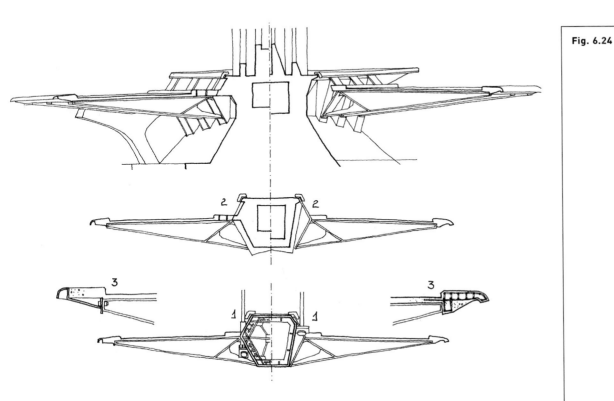

Fig. 6.24 | The cross section of the roadway along the pedestal and the main deck as originally conceived by Calatrava (right) and as actually built (left). The original section of the steel box (1) resembled an animal skull, with the cable stays anchored to short brackets springing outside the box. The wider, more circular box section as built has a greater torsional strength. The cantilevered roadways were first designed to be suspended from hollow steel hangers (2), allowing light to reach beneath the deck. Roadway supports and cable anchors are integrated into the later box design, and natural light reaches under the deck through skylights in the roadway slabs. The roadway's edges (3) were first designed as curved precast concrete elements; they were built of steel bolted to the deck's cantilevered wings. The Y-shaped support of the post-tensioned slabs was not included in the original design.

6.3.6
CONSTRUCTION CHANGES
ON THE DECK

Modifications to Calatrava's original design of the deck were initiated by the construction companies (fig. 6.24). Calatrava first designed the cross section of the steel box to echo the shape of the steel wings, rather reminiscent of the shape of a skull (see also fig. 3.1). The hexagonal cross section of the box was to have had four primary sides, with two smaller sides adjacent to the top. The box was considerably wider at the top than at the bottom, providing ample space for the pedestrian walkway; the upright sides were nearly perpendicular, providing a symmetry with the shape of the wings. The nearly vertical sides allowed plenty of light to pass between the box and the roadway, while at the location of the wings, bent steel elements in the form of ribs were attached to the box to hang the wings at a distance from the box itself, emphasizing the organic structure of the spine and the ribs. The cable stays were designed to be supported on steel plates outside the box.

The original design had to be modified during design development because it was particularly weak at the connection between the cable stays and the box. The anchoring of the cable stays within the box dictated most of the other changes.

The new design of the box retains its hexagonal shape but provides a more uniform distribution of its mass around the center and possesses increased torsional stiffness and strength. The anchoring tubes pass through the sides of the box to ensure sound anchoring of the cables. The top of each steel wing is connected directly to the prominent edges of the hexagon. The pedestal follows the new shape of the box, with an edge at the same level as the edge of the hexagon. The steel anchors spring from that edge and the steel wings along the pedestal connect directly to those anchors, touching the pedestal.

The new design does not achieve as organic a shape as the original, and it compresses the space between the deck and the box. Although it offers solid support to the steel wings, it allows less light to pass under the bridge. Further, although it keeps the top side of the box wider than the lower side, the difference is much smaller and visually less satisfactory.

Initially, the outer edges of the roadways were designed to be made from prefabricated reinforced concrete elements, without the use of steel brackets. The prefabricated elements would supply the formwork for the slabs at the edges of the roadways. However, such a construction was more difficult than the one eventually adopted, as it would not provide the required stability during the positioning of the steel wings. Furthermore, since the edge of the roadway defines the edge of the bridge, anything less than a perfect edge would affect the visual quality of the bridge; and the precast concrete elements would be more difficult to make perfect than the steel brackets.

The original design proposed building the last segment of the deck that spans the transverse roadway in back of the pylon without the Y-shaped elements. However, intermediate structural supports were required for the slabs at the side of the bridge, and the cantilevering wings were not sufficient at this point due to the increasing length of the cantilever. Thus, a pair of ground-based supports was introduced in place of the last pair of cantilevering wings.

6.4
THE PYLON

The pylon was made of reinforced concrete, placed in steel caissons that constituted a permanent formwork and defined the pylon's shape (fig. 6.25). The pylon has an interior stairway that provides access to the anchors of the cable stays and to an enclosed observation platform at the top.

6.4.1
GEOMETRY OF THE PYLON

The pylon is 134.25 m high, reaching 141.25 m above water level. It is inclined 58° with the horizontal, and the shape of its cross section changes along its length. The solid horizontal area of the pylon just above the pedestal is 110 m², decreasing to 44 m² at the top of the pylon. Table 4.4 gives the solid cross-sectional area perpendicular to the axis of the pylon.

All sections follow the basic hexagonal shape of the steel box of the deck, but significantly magnified. In an effort to soften the long sharp edges along the north and south sides of the pylon, two recesses have been introduced, 600 mm wide and 250 mm deep (see the plan of the steel caisson in fig. 6.26). The back of the pylon is recessed 900 mm to provide a protected space for the anchoring of the cable stays. The front of the pylon has a trapezoidal extrusion that pronounces the axis of the bridge, while it increases the stiffness of the pylon to withstand the bending moments from the cable stays, and offers a visual separation between the anchorings of the north and south cables of each pair (see fig. 6.29). All the edges of the upper part of the pylon, i.e., over 34.15 m above water level, run in straight lines.

As a result of the recesses and extrusions on the hexagon, the pylon has several surfaces. Some of those surfaces are inclined planes, like the back of the pylon. However, most of the surfaces of the pylon are hyperbolic paraboloids, defined by two edges of straight lines that do not lie on the same plane.

6.4.2
CONSTRUCTION OF THE PYLON

Sixteen main steel caissons were used to construct the pylon, each 7.30 m high. A caisson was fabricated in situ on top of the pedestal to provide the transition from the pedestal to the body of the py-

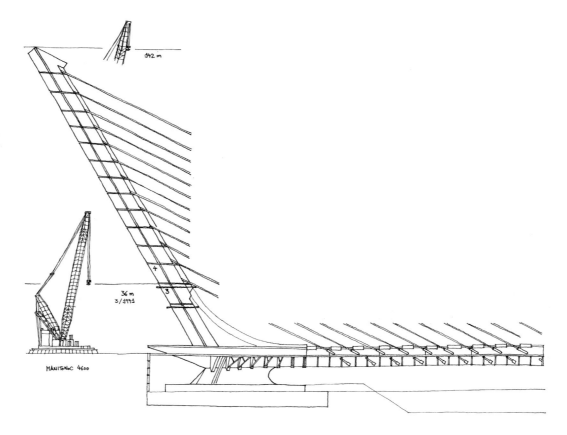

Fig. 6.25 The Manitowoc 4600 crane positioning the third caisson of the pylon in March 1991. The crane is built to the required working height of 36 m. Starting with the fourth caisson, the cable stays will counterbalance the weight of the pylon with that of the deck. The crane will be expanded to reach its final working height of 141.25 m without changing its position on the site.

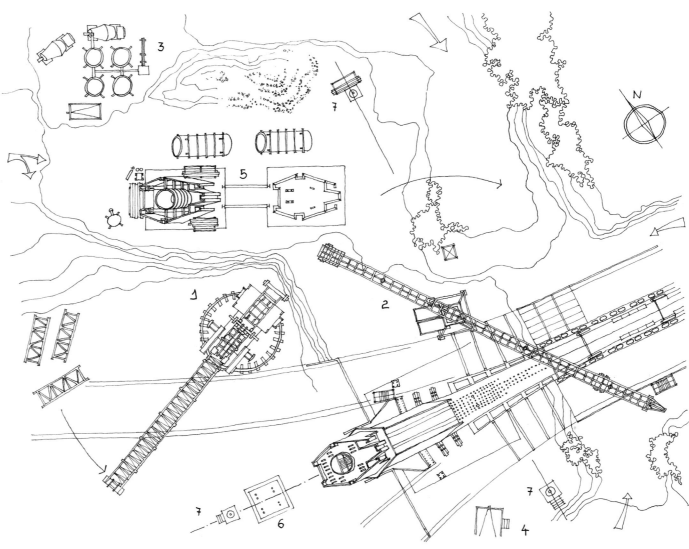

Fig. 6.26	An aerial view of the construction site on the west bank of the river. The large extensible crane on the left (1), used for the construction of the pylon, will reach above the top of the pylon. The smaller crane on the right (2) is used for the construction of the roadways and the deck-pylon connection. The site's storage area and concrete plant are located to the north (3), while the offices are on the south (4). The steel caissons of the pylon are transported in segments and assembled on site (5). The caisson's exterior steel plates, welding platforms, interior stairway, and reinforcing steel are all assembled on two templates before lifting the element to its final position on the pylon. A foundation for the cable-lifting winch (6) is built behind the pylon. Various surveying reference points are used for accurate positioning (7).

lon. A last caisson was placed on top to form the head of the pylon. The 16 main steel caissons were prefabricated in three pieces each and brought to the site by ground transportation. At the site (fig. 6.26), those pieces were welded to form a single caisson and all the steel parts were attached to it, including the scaffolding for welding it to the previously positioned caisson, the reinforcement bars, the anchors for the cable stays, and the interior stairway. The caissons were painted white before installation, except for a 50 mm unpainted zone along their edges, reserved for welding. Each caisson was raised by a Manitowoc 4600 crane and positioned on top of the already constructed part of the pylon (figs. 6.27, 6.28).

The capacity of the crane corresponding to the configuration of each caisson is given in table 6.1. The steel caissons were quite heavy, with the third caisson being the heaviest at 991 kN (table 6.2). After placement, hydraulic jacks put each caisson in its exact location, being surveyed from two observation towers. After each caisson was verified to be in its exact position, it was spot-welded to the previous caisson to allow removal of the crane support. It was then welded along its entire perimeter and along its stiffening diaphragms to prevent deformations from the 7.30 m high hydraulic pressure from the freshly placed concrete. The scaffolding used during the welding stayed on the steel caissons until the very last coat of paint had been applied.

The massive steel reinforcement in the pylon runs both along the axis of the pylon and on the planes of the cross sections. High-strength steel bars up to 32 mm in diameter constitute the longitudinal steel at the lower part of the pylon; at the upper part the maximum diameter decreases to 25 mm.

The stairway inside the pylon provides access to the cable anchorings and to the top of the pylon. The steel stairway was prefabricated and enclosed in steel tubes, in segments of 7.30 m, equal to the height of the corresponding steel caissons (see fig. 6.17). The stairway begins inside the first caisson, with a door at the back of the pylon at the level of the pedestrian walkway. Until the ninth caisson, the cylindrical stairway tube has an interior diameter of 4 m. In the upper seven caissons the diameter of the tube decreases to 2 m. The tube is situated along the axis of the pylon, following the same inclination as the pylon. Thus, its horizontal section is elliptic. The 4 m tube produces a horizontal ellipse with a long axis of 4.66 m, while the smaller tube produces an ellipse with a long axis of 2.33 m.

The concrete was pumped after each caisson and stairway tube were welded to the caisson below and all the reinforcing steel was inspected. The concrete mix was extensively studied to identify the right consistency of sand, gravel, and admixtures to pump from the base to the top of the pylon. A Schwing BLP 1200 HDR pumped the concrete to a height of 115 m at a rate of 35 m³/h. The pumping hose was located inside the stairway opening. The geometry of each caisson is such that the center of gravity is within the base, so that the caisson was able to support itself when filled with wet concrete. After the concrete hardened, the cable stays were placed on that segment of the pylon, and the next

| **Fig. 6.27** | A view of the pylon, the Manitowoc 4600 crane, and the cable-lifting winch as of August 26, 1991. Thirteen of the pylon's seventeen caissons are in place. Some of the temporary access and welding platforms have been removed. |

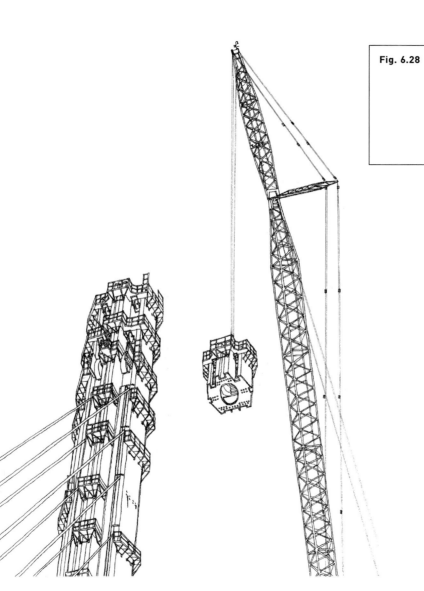

Fig. 6.28 | Lifting and positioning of the four-teenth steel caisson at the top of the pylon. Prior to the lifting opera-tion, the caisson is fully painted and assembled on the ground, including welding platforms, steel reinforce-ment, and the interior stairway.

Table 6.1 Capacity of the Manitowoc 4600 S-IV Ringer Series III 63 Boom corresponding to its configuration for the caissons of the pylon.

Caisson	Boom (m)	Secondary Boom (m)	Maximum distance (m)	Weight capacity (kN)	Minimum distance (m)	Weight capacity (kN)
1–9	91.4		91.4	615	22.8	2,489
10–11	115.8		91.4	374	28.9	1,503
12–16	115.8	36.5	128.0	231	38.1	906

Table 6.2 Weights of the segments of the deck and the caissons of the pylon.

Segment	Deck steel (kN)	Total (kN)	Caisson	Pylon steel (kN)	Total (kN)
1	1,128	7,936	0 + 1	903	9,947
2	3,120	11,272	2	795	11,321
3	2,914	8,240	3	991	12,459
4	2,727	7,652	4	863	14,391
5	2,815	7,671	5	922	11,625
6	2,982	7,956	6	755	11,036
7	2,943	7,868	7	716	10,565
8	2,649	6,494	8	638	9,830
Total	21,278	65,089	9	618	10,242
			10	559	11,036
			11	559	10,428
			12	559	9,771
			13	520	9,378
			14	540	8,898
			15	530	8,466
			16	579	7,583
			Head	451	1,422
			Total	11,497	168,398

caisson was positioned and welded (figs. 6.29, 6.30). Last, the pylon head was installed and welded on top of the sixteenth caisson (fig. 6.31). The head of the pylon does not support cables. Its lower section is filled with concrete to form the base of the observation platform; it also serves as the pinnacle of a sculptural element, with its two round decorative openings for nighttime illumination.

6.4.3
TRANSITION ELEMENT BETWEEN PYLON AND DECK

The transition element between the deck and the pylon has a footprint 32 m long, from the center of the pylon toward the deck. In elevation, it makes a smooth curve that ends just before the first pair of cables, 34.15 m above water level (fig. 6.32). This curved transition element, made of reinforced concrete placed in a permanent steel formwork (fig. 6.33), visually describes the moment connection of the deck and the pylon and the integration of the two elements that form the bridge. It facilitates formally the diversion of the roadway to embrace the pylon's pedestal.

The transition piece is symmetrical along the longitudinal plane of the bridge and is defined by nine edges on each side. Surfaces oriented in a general east-west direction are close to vertical, while the surfaces with north-south orientation are cylindrical with circular cross sections.

6.4.4
CONSTRUCTION CHANGES ON THE PYLON

Like the original design of the deck, that of the pylon was modified by the construction companies (fig. 6.34). As a piece of concrete, the pylon was designed to be a sculptural element, incorporating the signature curves of Calatrava's designs. Concrete's plasticity allows the designer to shape it in massive forms, almost free of constraints. Among the elements of the bridge, the pylon was the only major component designed to be constructed in concrete. However, an exposed concrete pylon introduced major construction and structural problems. First, the inclined shape of the pylon with its changing cross sections and massive quantities of concrete made quite difficult the building of a changing formwork. Then, it required the very dense reinforcement of 794 longitudinal bars of 32 mm diameter in addition to many more bars of 20 mm, as well as stirrups. It would also have been hard to maintain a high quality for the exposed concrete and to fashion sharp straight edges 135 m long. In its original form the pylon was also subject to large bending moments, as a result of the changing live loads acting on the bridge, and cracks could have developed on surfaces that were subject to tensile stresses. At the suggestion of the contractors, Carlos Alonso-Cobo, who was in charge of the design development for the reinforced concrete elements of the bridge, modified the design of the pylon to include steel caissons. The steel caissons significantly reduced the required reinforcement, served as the formwork during construction, and provided the smooth outer surface of the pylon. The original geometry of the pylon was simplified for the fabrication of the steel caissons, and many of the original curves were substituted with straight lines. So, despite efforts to maintain the designer's intentions, the new form of the pylon is not as pleasing as would have been the pylon shown in the original drawings and models.

6.5
CABLE STAYS

The original design of the bridge with the inclined pylon had 17 pairs of cable stays. These were reduced to 13 pairs during design development, eliminating the cable stays closest to the pedestal.

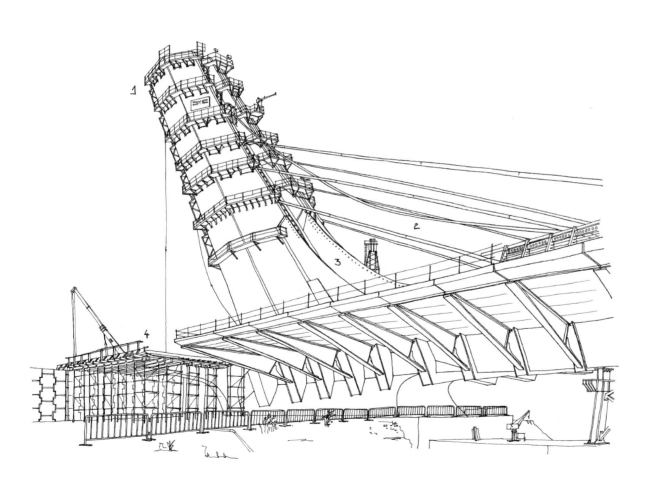

Fig. 6.29 | Perspective showing the erection of the pylon, the tensioning of the cables, and the completion of the roadways. The eighth steel caisson of the pylon has been positioned (1). The welding platforms of all caissons remain in place. The first three pairs of the cable stays (corresponding to caissons 4, 5, and 6) have already been tightened. The south cable stay for the seventh caisson is being pulled into its lower anchor (2). The first steel plates forming the curving connection between deck and pylon are being welded (3). The cantilevering roadways have been completed. The formwork for the post-tensioned concrete slabs connecting the roadways with the abutments is being assembled (4). The abutment is built with a system of interlocking concrete panels.

Fig. 6.30 Formwork for the north post-tensioned slab. The view shows the abutment support in the foreground and the roadway slab in the background. As of July 26, 1991, eight caissons had already been assembled on the pylon, and the 700 kN winch (1) lifts one of the fourth pair of cable stays. The elevator (2) moves toward the fourth caisson.

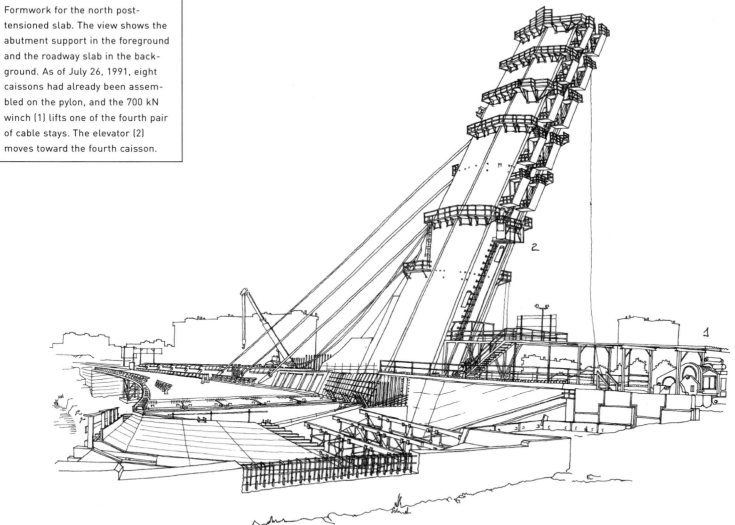

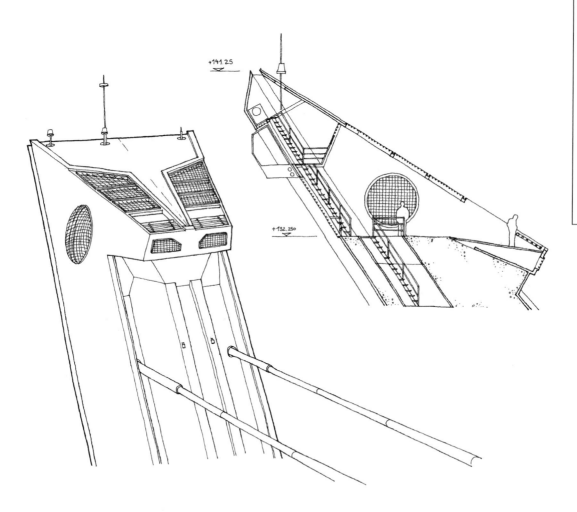

+141.25

+141.25

+132.250

Fig. 6.31 | The head of the pylon. Unlike the sixteen caissons below, the pylon's top caisson is open and empty. It features an observation platform and two large round windows protected by safety grills. At a level of 141.25 m, it is by far the highest point in the city of Seville—a magnificent vantage point over the Expo '92 site and the metropolitan area. A plan to convert the pylon into a public observation deck was unrealized. After construction was completed, the temporary elevator was removed, and now the head of the pylon can only be accessed through the interior stairway.

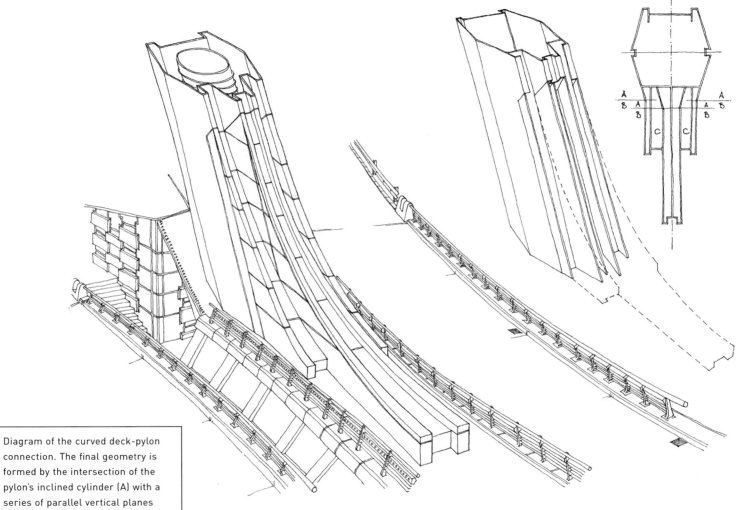

Fig. 6.32 Diagram of the curved deck-pylon connection. The final geometry is formed by the intersection of the pylon's inclined cylinder (A) with a series of parallel vertical planes (B and C).

Fig. 6.33 Concrete being pumped into the deck-pylon connection. An articulated pumping arm (1) is used to fill the connection with concrete. Workers assemble the remaining steel plates from multiple temporary platforms (2). Part of the interior guard rail of the roadway has already been welded in place (3). A temporary stair connects the roadway with the pedestrian walkway.

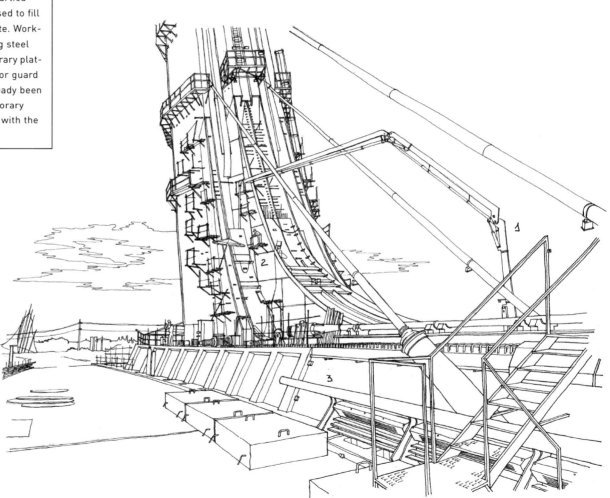

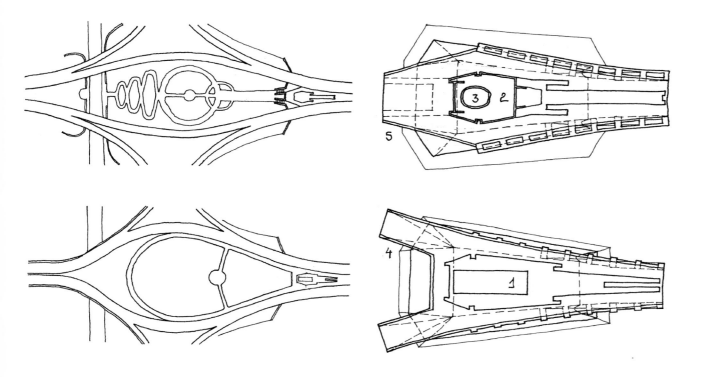

Fig. 6.34 A comparison of the original (bottom) and final (top) cross section of the pylon and the layout of the pedestrian walkway. The original pylon was a continuous concrete section, to be constructed with a sliding formwork (1). The final section, however, features steel plate caissons and concrete filling (2). A tubular steel element forms the interior stairway (3). Changes in the design of the circulation node leading to the bridge prompted the modification of the pedestrian walkway around the pylon. Originally, the pedestrian walkway split in two after clearing the pylon (4), while in the final layout the walkway merges again (5). The landscaped area behind the pylon was also different in the original design.

The cables were made of Flo Bond epoxy-coated strands manufactured in the United States by Florida Wire and Cable. Dywidag Systems International (DSI) carried out the in-situ assembly of the cables, their installation, and their post-tensioning. The Alamillo Bridge was the first cable-stayed bridge in the world for which the cables were fabricated in situ using epoxy-coated strands, and then moved to their final position.

Each cable is anchored with a passive support on the back of the pylon and an active support on the deck. The cables were installed in pairs, first the north and then the south cable, and then they were tensioned together. A single cable alone can support the corresponding dead weight of the bridge, allowing the other cable to be replaced if necessary.

6.5.1
FABRICATION OF THE CABLES

The nominal diameter of each Flo Bond epoxy-coated strand is 0.60 inches (15.24 mm), made of 270-grade high-strength steel (270,000 lb per square inch = 39.15 MPa). The area of the cross section is 140 mm² and the breaking load per strand is 261 kN. Each strand is made of seven wires; the diameter of the center wire is 5.18 mm

and that of the six peripheral wires is 4.98 mm. The strand itself is epoxy-coated and all the gaps among the wires are filled with epoxy, which serves as a cushion. The strands were shipped in reels of 2,620 m from the manufacturer. In addition to being used for cable-stayed bridges, these epoxy-coated strands are widely used as tendons for post-tensioned concrete structures.

The first twelve pairs of cables in the Alamillo Bridge were made of 60 strands each. The two longest cables of the thirteenth pair have only 45 strands. The cables were fabricated on site on special beds that were constructed along both sides of the pedestrian walkway. Supported on steel beams, the construction beds were equipped with wooden forms with which to make the hexagonal cross section of each cable (see fig. 6.41F). The strands were positioned in those beds either one by one or in pairs. When all the strands for a cable were in place, plastic spacers were installed every 2 m, in order to maintain the shape of the cable's cross section and to position the cable within its protective tube.

The white protective polyethylene tube was installed next. The tube has an outside diameter of 207 mm and is 11 mm thick. It is made of a 3 mm exposed layer of white polyethylene bonded on an 8 mm black polyethylene tube. Segments of 10 m

long tube were aligned with the cable, at the pylon end of the cable. With the help of winches, each tube segment was pulled along the cable and then connected to the next 10 m segment. The entire cable was thus covered with the protective tube except for 10 m on each end. The expansion coefficient of polyethylene is ten times higher than that of steel, so a telescopic tube made of the same material was installed later to protect the end of the cable and allow dilatation between the cable and the polyethylene tube.

6.5.2
INSTALLATION OF THE CABLES

The cables were installed after the concrete had hardened in the corresponding caisson of the pylon, while the caisson above was being welded (fig. 6.35). By that time, the deck had been completed and was supported on the scaffolding on the riverbed. The fabrication bed served as the sliding track for pulling each cable to its position (fig. 6.36). The surface of the track was covered with Teflon to reduce the friction between the cable and the track. An extension of the sliding track was constructed on the surface of the pylon, also covered with Teflon. Two temporary leading supports were installed close to the anchoring points and the

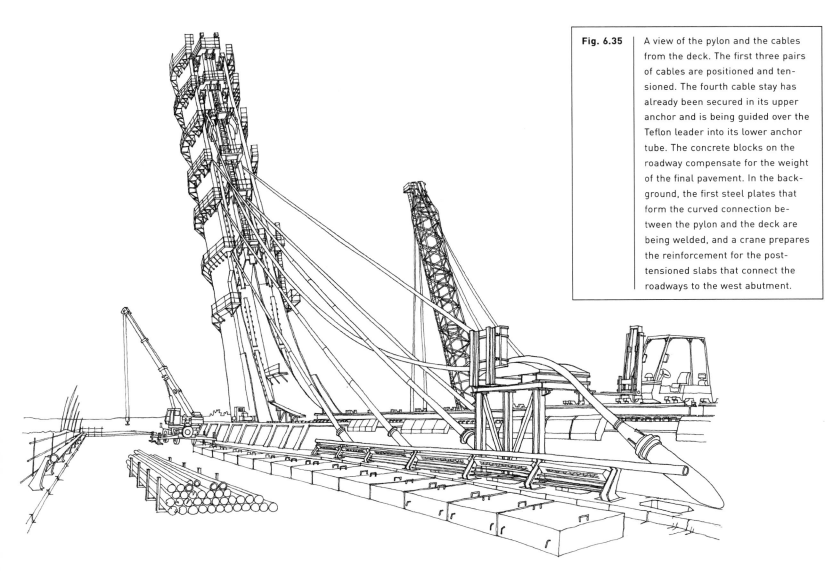

Fig. 6.35 A view of the pylon and the cables from the deck. The first three pairs of cables are positioned and tensioned. The fourth cable stay has already been secured in its upper anchor and is being guided over the Teflon leader into its lower anchor tube. The concrete blocks on the roadway compensate for the weight of the final pavement. In the background, the first steel plates that form the curved connection between the pylon and the deck are being welded, and a crane prepares the reinforcement for the post-tensioned slabs that connect the roadways to the west abutment.

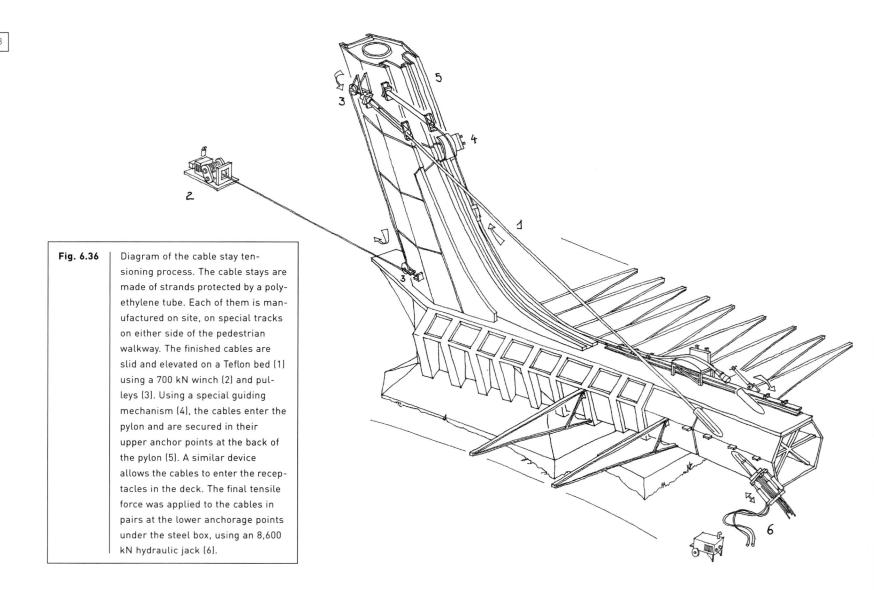

Fig. 6.36 | Diagram of the cable stay tensioning process. The cable stays are made of strands protected by a polyethylene tube. Each of them is manufactured on site, on special tracks on either side of the pedestrian walkway. The finished cables are slid and elevated on a Teflon bed (1) using a 700 kN winch (2) and pulleys (3). Using a special guiding mechanism (4), the cables enter the pylon and are secured in their upper anchor points at the back of the pylon (5). A similar device allows the cables to enter the receptacles in the deck. The final tensile force was applied to the cables in pairs at the lower anchorage points under the steel box, using an 8,600 kN hydraulic jack (6).

cable was slid on top of those leaders. The lower leader was positioned close to the pass-through tube of the steel box, the upper leader just before the pass-through tube in the pylon.

A small guiding cable was attached to a 700 kN winch on the back of the pylon and, through pulleys, it went above the anchoring tube in the pylon and was connected to a larger guiding cable, which in turn pulled the cable stay (fig. 6.37). The winch pulled the guiding cable and raised the cable to its upper anchoring point at the pylon. Then the cable was anchored permanently in the pylon and the guiding cable was released.

On the deck side, the shorter cables were driven through their anchoring tubes using a crane. The longer cables were pulled using hydraulic jacks.

6.5.3
TENSIONING THE CABLES

The cables were post-tensioned in pairs, immediately following their installation and were not tensioned again. Table 4.7 shows the tensioning force for each pair of cables. The post-tensioning was achieved in seven sequential loading steps, during each of which the change in the length of the cable was checked for consistency with the applied

tension force. The length of the cable was calculated by surveying the anchoring points at the pylon and at the deck, taking into account temperature effects as well. Further checks were performed the following day for final approval of the status of that pair of cables.

Finally, the last 10 m of the cables at each end were grouted using a cementitious material that protected the connections between the strands and the anchoring heads, which had exposed steel surfaces. The main length of the cables did not require protection because the strands were covered with epoxy.

After all the cables were tensioned, the temporary supports of the deck and the earth embankment were removed from the riverbed (fig. 6.38).

6.5.4
REPLACEMENT OF DAMAGED CABLES

While the pylon's head was being welded during the installation of the last pair of cables, the cable on the north side of the bridge caught fire. Several strands in the sixth, eleventh, and thirteenth cables on the north side of the bridge were damaged, although the damage was confined to the end of the cable stays next to the pylon, where the telescopic protection had not yet been installed.

All three cable stays affected by the fire had to be replaced. The tension in the thirteenth cable was released strand by strand since the end of the strands had not been cut yet. In the other two cables, the strands had been cut; a special device was used to release the tension in the cable as a whole, by first providing a connection with 60 strands to provide the additional length for the hydraulic jack. Next, the replacement cables were installed according to the standard construction procedure that had been followed for the installation and tensioning of the cables.

6.6
FINISHES

The safety barriers for the vehicular traffic were designed by Calatrava following the specifications of MOPU. Their height is 825 mm above their base, or 962 mm above the surface of the roadway. They consist of a main cylindrical bar, 139 mm in diameter, that runs along the edges of the roadway, supported every 4 m by oblique massive elements that follow the slope of the top part of a hexagon (fig. 6.39). Three rectangular bars running parallel to the main cylindrical bar complete the safety barriers of the roadway.

Fig. 6.37 A cross section of the pylon showing the exterior welding platforms as well as the cable guiding system. The welding platforms (1) can be accessed through the permanent interior stairway (2) or through a temporary elevator running on tracks along the back of the pylon (3). Exterior ladders (4) lead from each of the elevator stops to the welding platform immediately above. Ladders on the front of the pylon connect other welding platforms. The cable stays are slid on a Teflon bed along the front of the pylon. The pulling cable crosses the pylon through an auxiliary horizontal tube in the upper part of the steel caisson (A). A special mechanism is used to align the sliding cable with the inclined anchoring tube. Once the cable stay reaches the lower opening of the anchoring tube, it is secured to the guiding system and released from the pulling cable. Then it is rotated and pulled through the anchoring tube (B) toward its final position (C). The illustration shows the positioning of the third cable stay in the sixth caisson.

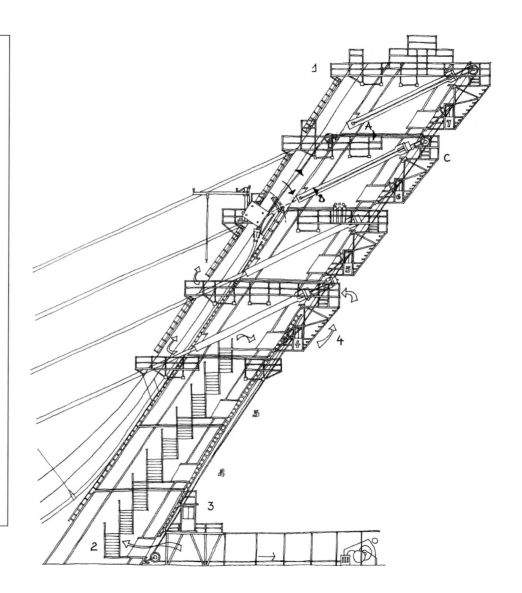

Fig. 6.38 | A view under the deck of the bridge, near completion. The deck's temporary support structures have been removed, and the riverbed is being cleared. Multiple cables forming each of the cable stays hang from the deck after the final tensioning operation. Over the deck, concrete is being pumped into the curved deck-pylon connection.

Fig. 6.39 Details of roadway curbs and guard rails. The drawings show the pre-cast concrete slab formwork of the roadways (1), the cast-in-place concrete slabs and curbs (2), the steel skylight forms (3), and the side of the deck's steel box (4). The guard rails are welded to steel plates (5) embedded in the cast-in-place concrete of the curb. The rail integrates a low-level light fixture with grills facing the roadway (6) and round openings on the other side (7).

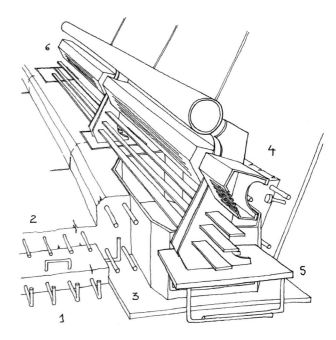

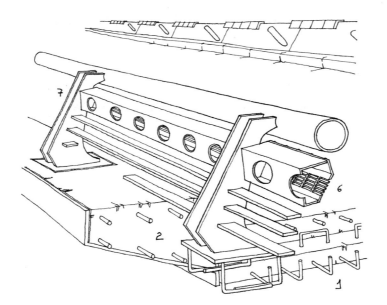

The pedestrian railings (fig. 6.40) are similar to the safety barriers for the vehicles. They are 880 mm high and narrower than the traffic barriers; the top cylindrical bar is 84 mm in diameter, made of stainless steel. Below this bar there are four additional prismatic bars to form the railing.

There are no vertical posts with light fixtures on the bridge. All the light fixtures have either been integrated into the safety barriers and the railings or attached inconspicuously to the body of the bridge. The light fixtures incorporated into the safety barriers are located immediately below the main bar. They are continuous along the roadway and contain fluorescent light tubes. The fixtures on the outer edge of the roadway have round holes to cast light outside the bridge, and a grilled surface to illuminate the roadway. Those on the inner edge have an identical geometry, the round holes in this case illuminating the top part of the main steel box of the deck. The interior safety barrier is positioned close to the skylights of the deck, partially obstructing the natural light reaching under the bridge. At night, however, the skylights illuminate the box and the wings under the roadway, emphasizing the structural skeleton of the deck.

The light fixtures of the pedestrian railings are identical to those of the safety barriers, illuminating the pedestrian walkway and outlining the shape of the bridge. More light fixtures are positioned under the bridge to illuminate the lower part of the deck, and at various positions to illuminate the pylon and the cables. The head of the pylon is illuminated internally, emphasizing the two large round openings that resemble two big eyes at night.

6.7
CHANGES IN THE ARCHITECT'S DESIGN

More often than not, original designs are modified during design development. In most cases, the modifications are justified on technological grounds. Either the available technology cannot support the proposed design solutions, or it has not been tested adequately and its reliability is unknown, or the specific contractor has no experience with the technology required by the specific design. Often, time, cost, and convenience of construction are driving reasons for changes and, under those circumstances, the intentions of the designer are given a lower priority (Diaz-Hermidas, 1994).

The Alamillo Bridge serves as an example of contractors' particular sensitivity to the intentions of the designer. Changes to the architectural drawings that had been used for bidding were inevitable, either for reasons of structural integrity or to speed the construction operations and meet the deadline of the opening of Expo '92. The modifications that were introduced to the original design of the Alamillo Bridge during design development and construction retained the spirit of the architectural intentions, although they changed the construction of the bridge (fig. 6.41).

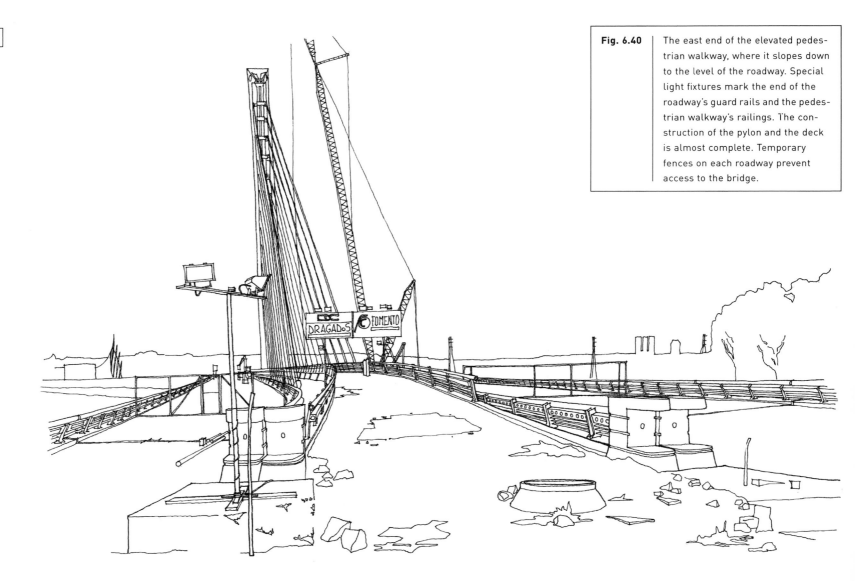

Fig. 6.40 | The east end of the elevated pedestrian walkway, where it slopes down to the level of the roadway. Special light fixtures mark the end of the roadway's guard rails and the pedestrian walkway's railings. The construction of the pylon and the deck is almost complete. Temporary fences on each roadway prevent access to the bridge.

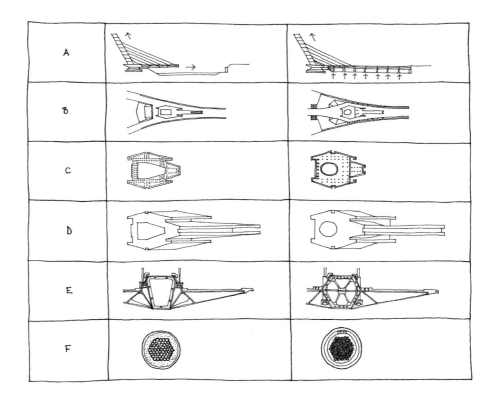

Fig. 6.41 | A summary of the main design changes made during the construction process. The left column presents the original designs, while the right column shows the built conditions. As a result of schedule constraints and for increased construction efficiency, the original cantilevered construction process was abandoned (A). In the final design the pedestrian walkway merges again after clearing the pylon (B). The original pylon design was a reinforced concrete structure built with a sliding formwork. The actual pylon, however, is a composite concrete and steel structure, the steel caisson serving as formwork into which the concrete is later pumped (C). The structural capacity of the steel shell allows substantially reduced interior reinforcement. The curving connection between the pylon and the deck, a continuous warped element in the original design, was finally built with intersecting flat steel plates (D). The original skull-shaped steel box of the deck was modified to integrate cable stay anchors and deck wing supports into a single element (E). Finally, the individual strands forming the cable stays were self-protected with an epoxy coating and did not require protective injections (F).

7 EPILOGUE

The bold shape of the inclined pylon of the Alamillo Bridge (fig. 7.1) has made it a dominant part of Seville's cityscape, visible from several streets downtown (fig. 7.2), and the architectural emphasis of the details have made the Alamillo Bridge a contemporary symbol, as integral a part of Seville as the Giralda (fig. 7.3).[1]

Excitement over the bridge began as early as the commission was awarded. The bridge had been a focal point of architectural and engineering debates in Andalucía, as well as in the rest of Spain. Both the press and the locals often referred to it as "the harp," or as "the Trojan horse," a response to both the shape of the pylon's head and the hollowness of the pylon. It has also been called "the aircraft carrier," comparing the deck of the bridge to the hull of an aircraft carrier. Finally, some see it as a phallic symbol dominating the cityscape of Seville. At one time, the Junta de Andalucía considered naming the bridge Puente Colón (Columbus Bridge) to honor Columbus and the quincentennial of his discovery of the Americas.

The completion of the bridge was celebrated vividly, gratifying those who had believed in it and succeeded in making it a reality. The Junta had offered the leadership and vision to place art above cost, driven by a strong desire to produce monumental architecture, and took the risks to make the project possible. Manuel Chaves, the President of the Junta de Andalucía, stated in his inaugural speech for the bridge on February 29, 1992: "The Alamillo Bridge is the most important piece of work that the Junta de Andalucía has built on the occasion of Expo '92. . . . The bridge does not simply offer [transportation] service to the city, it is one of the most important architectural monuments that will remain after Expo '92 is over."

The people of Seville share the feelings of Manuel Chaves. Soon after its opening, the Alamillo Bridge became the pride of the neighborhood. People like to walk and meet on the bridge and to enjoy the relaxing views of the river and the city. By designing a monumental bridge, Calatrava gave them an urban space as attractive as his famous Felipe II Bridge had offered five years earlier, in the neighborhood of Bach de Roda in Barcelona. The special consideration of the pedestrian walkways, as well as the provision for pedestrian access to the river banks and the attention to finishing the surfaces under the bridge, have succeeded in making the bridge an extension of its Seville neighborhood and part of the urban context.

| Fig. 7.1 | An aerial view of the Alamillo Bridge, with a view toward the installations for Expo '92 on Cartuja Island. Photo by FCP, S.A. |

Fig. 7.2 | The pylon of the Alamillo Bridge seen from a narrow street in downtown Seville.

Fig. 7.3 | The Alamillo Bridge in the cityscape of Seville, next to the Giralda.

APPENDIX A **DATA SHEET**

Owner	Junta de Andalucía. Consejería de Obras Públicas y Transportes. Dirección General de Carreteras
Designer	Santiago Calatrava-Valls
Engineers	Angel Aparicio-Bencoechea (general analysis) Carlos Alonso-Cobo (reinforced and prestressed concrete, and foundation) José Ramón Atienza-Reales (steel structures)
Construction	"Puente del Alamillo," temporary association of the construction companies Fomento de Construcciónes y Contratas SA and Dragados y Construcciónes SA, both with headquarters in Madrid
Steel manufacturer	British Steel
Steel fabrication	MEGUSA (Metalúrgica de Guadalquivir, SA), and SAMICA, both based in Seville
Cable strands manufacturer	Florida Wire & Cable, USA
Cable assembly and pre-tensioning	DSI, Germany
Instrumentation	Vicrusa SA, Seville
Official opening date	February 29, 1992

Dimensions	Abutment to abutment	220 m
	Center of pylon to east abutment	200 m
	Clear span	186 m
	Elevation of pedestrian walkway	15 m above water level 1.80 m above the roadway
	Elevation of roadway	13.20 m above water level
	Clearance of the bridge	10 m above water level
Foundation	54 piles	2 m in diameter, 47.5 m in depth, the last 26 m embedded in marl
Pylon	Composite structure	Steel and concrete, 16 caissons of approximately 7.30 m in height plus the head caisson
	Height of pylon	134.25 m above the foundation level 141.25 m above water level
	Base of pylon	7.30 m above water level
	Gross area of pylon	Variable, 55 m^2 perpendicular to its axis at elevation 76.15 m, 103.8 m^2 horizontal area
	Diameter of tube for interior stairway	4 m until elevation 76.15, and 2 m from elevation 76.15 until elevation 132.25 m
	Weight of pylon above pedestal	185 MN
	Weight of pile cap and pedestal	175 MN
	Inclination of the pedestal	32° with the vertical axis (58° with the horizontal axis)
Deck	Width of deck	32 m
	Width of pedestrian walkway	3.75 m
	Supports for box in construction	7

Deck (cont'd)	Assembly of steel box	8 segments, 6 segments of 24 m each, 9.50 m the first (close to the pylon), 21.30 m the last; total: 174.80 m
	Cantilevering wings	Every 4 m (total of 42 pairs of wings springing from the steel box, 8 steel wings springing from the base of the pylon)
	Depth of steel box	4.40 m
	Top of steel box	Variable from 3.75 to 6.394 m
	Bottom of steel box	Variable from 3.246 to 5.890 m
	Prefabricated concrete elements	100 mm thick
	Poured slab on deck	130 mm thick
	Weight of the deck	81 MN
Cables	13 pairs	
	Cable protection	Auto-protected epoxy-coated strands; outside protecting tube of polyethylene, diameter 200 mm
	Diameter of cables (nos. 1–12)	60 strands, 15.2 mm (0.60 inches) in diameter each; area of each cable 8,400 mm^2; weight of cable and tube 780 N/m
	Longest cables (no. 13)	292 m long, 45 strands 15.2 mm (0.60 inches) in diameter; area of each cable 6,300 mm^2; weight of cable and tube 600 N/m
Quantities of materials	Structural steel in deck	25 MN
	Structural steel in pylon	16 MN
	Concrete in pylon	7,000 m^3
	Concrete in deck, foundation, and abutments	10,100 m^3
	Reinforcing steel	28 MN
	Steel in cable stays	3,350 kN

Construction equipment	Crane for pylon	Maximum single weight 2.2 MN, Manitowoc 4600 series IV and ringer series III
	Crane for deck	Maximum single weight 1 MN, Manitowoc 4100
	Capacity of cable-tensioning hydraulic jack	8.6 MN
	Capacity of winch for cable installation	700 kN

APPENDIX B **CONSTRUCTION COSTS**

Element or operation	Units	Unit price ($US)	Cost ($US)
Excavation (m³)	21,735	4.35	94,546
Earth fills (m³)	18,586	5.81	107,982
Drainage of deck	62	72.75	4,510
Reinforcing steel AEH-500, corrugated bars (kg)	2,119,103	0.78	1,652,900
Reinforcing steel AEH-500, threaded bars (kg)	307,810	1.25	384,762
Cable strands (kg)	335,932	8.50	2,855,422
Concrete H-100 (m³)	177	61.52	10,894
Concrete H-200 (m³)	198	75.19	14,861
Concrete H-300 for pedestal (m³)	2,099	87.50	183,689
Concrete H-300 for abutment (m³)	2,595	97.00	251,715
Concrete H-350 for pylon (m³)	6,981	140.00	977,326
Concrete H-350 (m³)	1,123	98.20	110,274
Formwork for foundation and prestressed slabs (m²)	993	11.00	10,920
Formwork for curved or inclined elements except pylon (m²)	4,520	19.50	88,144
Unidirectional support for 750 tn and 100 mm displacement	2	4,500.00	9,000
Expansion joint of deck type C (+140 mm) (m)	58	1,800.00	104,400
Load test	1	14,900.00	14,900
Concrete H-350 for joints (m³)	2,519	112.44	283,239
Railing type 2.1 (m)	506	450.00	227,700
Railing type 2.2 (m)	620	222.00	137,640

Element or operation	Units	Unit price ($US)	Cost ($US)
Piles (m)	2,565	1,515.63	3,887,591
Piers constructed with bentonite (m)	416	683.25	284,505
Joint of deck, type B	29	737.00	21,373
Steel slabs with skylights	102	1,850.00	188,700
Prefabricated concrete planks for roadway slabs (m²)	4,468	95.20	425,354
Prefabricated concrete planks for retaining walls (m²)	752	352.00	264,584
Finish on formwork (m³)	6,265	2.50	15,663
Spherical support for 2200 tn	2	27,500.00	55,000
Post-tensioned strands (m)	9,001	3.05	27,452
Concrete H-250 (m³)	688	81.50	56,039
Concrete H-250 (m³)	753	90.00	67,789
Str. steel A52d (includes paint etc.) for steel wings (kg)	681,755	4.81	3,279,242
Str. steel A52d (includes paint etc.) for steel box (kg)	1,059,512	4.96	5,255,179
Str. steel A52d (includes paint etc.) for steel box (kg)	552,771	5.16	2,852,298
Str. steel A52d (includes paint etc.) for cable supports (kg)	119,600	6.93	828,828
Str. steel A52d (includes paint etc.) for pylon (kg)	1,591,256	8.39	13,350,640
Gate for Seville abutment	1	11,023.84	11,024
Pylon	2	60,397.60	120,795
Lightning protection	1	28,943.71	28,944
Total			**$38,545,823**

APPENDIX C SELECTED CONSTRUCTION DRAWINGS

A total of 367 construction drawings were prepared for the bridge. Thirteen of those construction drawings are included in this appendix.

Fig. C.1

Section of the pylon and the pedestal along their plane of symmetry. The drawing shows the geometry of the pedestal and the transition element between the deck and the pylon.

Fig. C.2

Section of the pylon along its plane of symmetry. The drawing shows the steel caissons, the pylon's head, and the anchoring points of the cables along the pylon. It also includes the coordinates of the cables.

Fig. C.3

Cross section of the pylon at elevations of 36 m and 76.15 m. The drawing includes a table with the data that define the geometry of all the steel caissons.

Fig. C.4

Section of the deck along its plane of symmetry. The drawing shows the segments of the prefabricated steel box, and the section of the river.

Fig. C.5

Geometry of the steel box of the deck. The drawing shows the plan from the top and from underneath and the elevation of the steel box, together with the data that define its geometry. Three typical cross sections are also included in the drawing.

Fig. C.6

Cross section of the deck, including information on the steel wings.

Fig. C.7

Cross section of the steel box at eight different locations, together with welding information.

Fig. C.8

Cross section of the pedestal on a vertical plane, showing the concrete part of the deck and the opening inside the pedestal. A detail shows the construction of the pedestrian walkway with the precast concrete pieces that define its edges.

Fig. C.9

Horizontal cross section of the pedestal showing the lower part of the pylon. At elevation 15.353 m above water level, the drawing shows the footprint of the transition element between the deck and the pylon.

Fig. C.10

Horizontal and vertical cross sections of the pylon at various elevations, showing the steel reinforcement inside the caissons.

Fig. C.11

The cable anchors on the pylon, in elevation, horizontal cross section, and cross section along the axis of the cable.

Fig. C.12

A cross section of the pedestal, showing the Y-shaped support element of the post-tensioned roadway slabs. On top of the Y-shaped element, the two supports for the post-tensioned roadway slabs are shown as extrusions of the element.

Fig. C.13

The park and the rotaries between the Alamillo Bridge and the Cartuja viaduct.

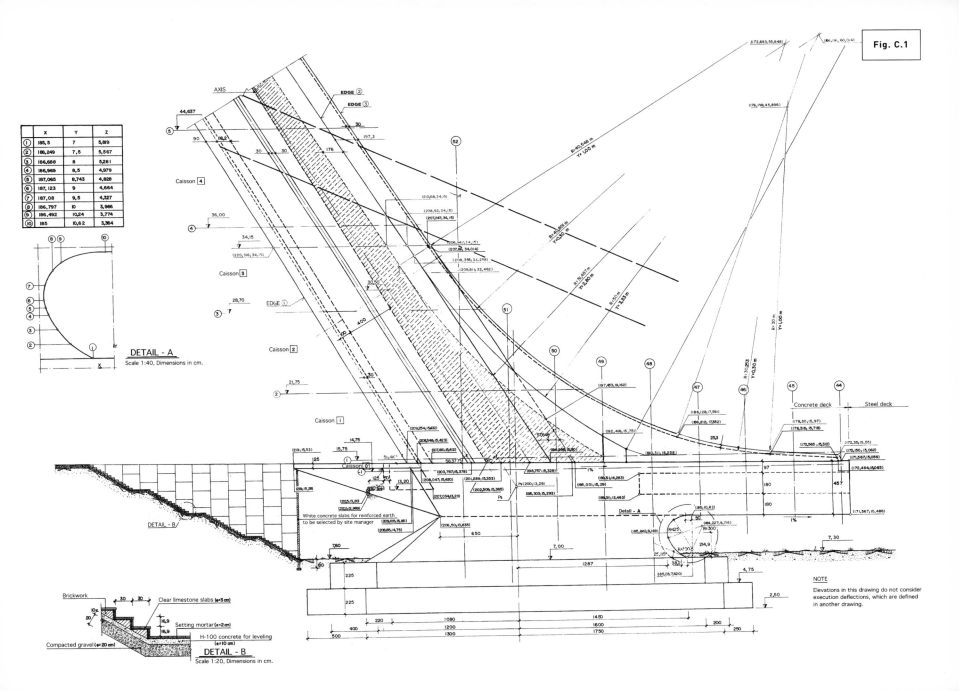

Fig. C.1

	X	Y	Z
①	185,5	7	5,819
②	186,249	7,5	5,567
③	186,688	8	5,281
④	186,969	8,5	4,979
⑤	187,065	8,743	4,828
⑥	187,123	9	4,664
⑦	187,08	9,5	4,327
⑧	186,797	10	3,966
⑨	186,492	10,24	3,774
⑩	185	10,62	3,364

DETAIL - A
Scale 1:40, Dimensions in cm.

DETAIL - B
Scale 1:20, Dimensions in cm.

Brickwork
Clear limestone slabs (e=3 cm)
Setting mortar (e=2 cm)
H-100 concrete for leveling (e=10 cm)
Compacted gravel (e=20 cm)

White concrete slabs for reinforced earth to be selected by site manager

Concrete deck   Steel deck

Caisson 4
Caisson 3
Caisson 2
Caisson 1
Caisson 0

AXIS
EDGE ②
EDGE ③
EDGE ①

NOTE
Elevations in this drawing do not consider execution deflections, which are defined in another drawing.

Fig. C.2

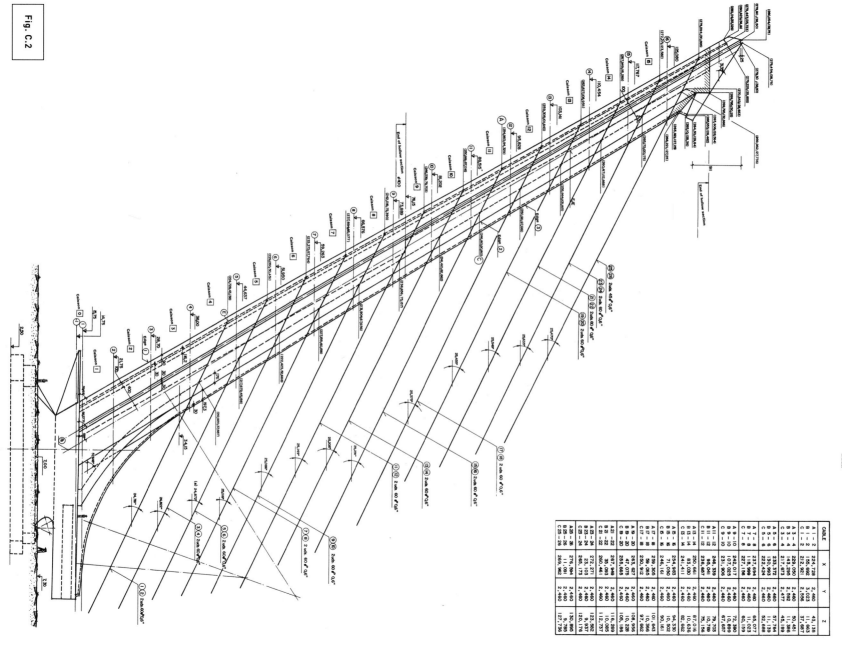

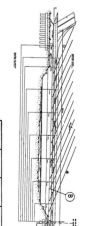

CABLE	X	Y	Z
A 1 — 2	224,728	2,460	43,135
B 1 — 2	195,692	3,023	11,663
C 1 — 2	212,921	2,556	37,687
A 3 — 4	229,050	2,460	50,451
B 3 — 4	143,295	2,592	11,396
C 3 — 4	217,673	2,477	45,189
A 5 — 6	233,372	2,460	57,764
B 5 — 6	130,993	2,460	11,139
C 5 — 6	222,424	2,460	52,686
A 7 — 8	237,694	2,460	65,077
B 7 — 8	118,999	2,460	11,023
C 7 — 8	227,194	2,460	60,139
A 9 — 10	242,017	2,460	72,390
B 9 — 10	107,025	2,460	10,789
C 9 — 10	231,906	2,460	67,657
A 11 — 12	246,339	2,460	79,703
B 11 — 12	95,041	2,460	10,502
C 11 — 12	236,687	2,460	75,146
A 13 — 14	250,661	2,460	87,016
B 13 — 14	83,030	2,460	10,636
C 13 — 14	241,411	2,460	82,662
A 15 — 16	254,983	2,460	94,330
B 15 — 16	71,050	2,460	10,228
C 15 — 16	246,161	2,460	90,161
A 17 — 18	259,305	2,460	101,643
B 17 — 18	59,065	2,460	10,366
C 17 — 18	250,912	2,460	97,682
A 19 — 20	263,627	2,460	108,956
B 19 — 20	47,075	2,460	10,229
C 19 — 20	255,665	2,460	105,186
A 21 — 22	267,949	2,460	116,269
B 21 — 22	35,093	2,460	10,085
C 21 — 22	260,461	2,460	112,757
A 23 — 24	272,271	2,460	123,582
B 23 — 24	23,103	2,460	9,937
C 23 — 24	265,173	2,460	120,176
A 25 — 26	276,594	2,460	130,895
B 25 — 26	11,091	2,460	9,785
C 25 — 26	269,962	2,460	127,736

Fig. C.3

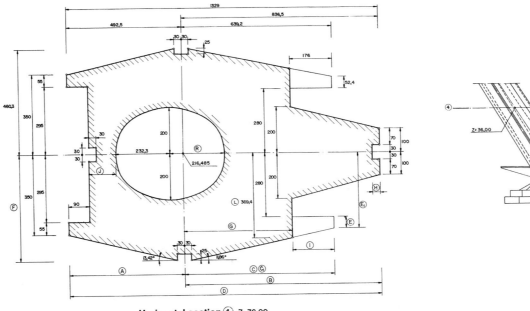

Horizontal section ④, Z= 36,00
Scale 1:50.-Dimensions in cm

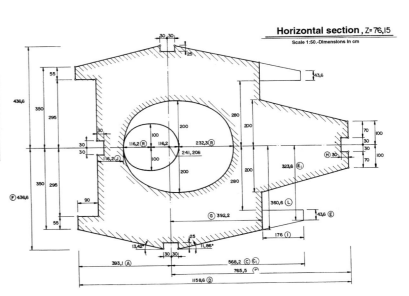

Horizontal section , Z= 76,15
Scale 1:50.-Dimensions in cm

SECTION	X	Z	A	B	C	D	E	F	G
-1	203.400	14.750	5.450	31.250	13.089	36.700	0.530	4.729	5.008
1	204.016	15.750	5.426	28.832	13.708	34.258	0.530	4.723	4.991
2	207.710	21.750	5.277	13.075	9.409	18.352	0.530	4.688	4.885
3	211.990	28.700	5.105	9.178	6.894	14.283	0.530	4.647	4.762
4	216.485	36.000	4.923	8.365	6.392	13.290	0.524	4.603	4.632
5	221.803	44.637	4.711	8.213	6.240	12.924	0.505	4.552	4.480
6	226.306	51.950	4.530	8.083	6.110	12.613	0.489	4.509	4.350
7	230.809	59.263	4.349	7.954	5.981	12.303	0.473	4.466	4.221
8	235.312	66.576	4.168	7.825	5.852	11.993	0.457	4.423	4.092
9	239.815	73.889	3.987	7.695	5.722	11.682	0.441	4.380	3.962
10	244.318	81.202	3.806	7.566	5.593	11.372	0.425	4.337	3.833
11	248.821	88.515	3.625	7.437	5.464	11.062	0.409	4.293	3.704
12	253.324	95.828	3.444	7.307	5.334	10.751	0.393	4.250	3.574
13	257.827	103.141	3.263	7.178	5.205	10.441	0.377	4.207	3.445
14	262.330	110.454	3.082	7.048	5.075	10.131	0.361	4.164	3.315
15	266.834	117.767	2.901	6.919	4.946	9.820	0.345	4.121	3.186
16	271.337	125.080	2.720	6.790	4.817	9.510	0.329	4.077	3.057

SECTION	Z	H	I	J	R	L	C1	E1	I1
-1	14.750	0.314	2.105	1.162	2.323	3.740	6.768	3.371	22.509
1	15.750	3.547	2.105	1.162	2.323	3.738	6.751	3.368	20.109
2	21.750	0.464	2.265	1.162	2.323	3.725	6.645	3.355	4.457
3	28.700	0.340	1.890	1.162	2.323	3.710	6.522	3.340	0.684
4	36.000	0.300	1.760	1.162	2.323	3.694	6.392	3.324	0.000
5	44.637	0.300	1.760	1.162	2.323	3.675	6.240	3.305	0.000
6	51.950	0.300	1.760	1.162	2.323	3.659	6.110	3.289	0.000
7	59.263	0.300	1.790	1.162	2.323	3.643	5.981	3.273	0.000
8	66.576	0.300	1.760	1.162	2.323	3.627	5.852	3.257	0.000
9	73.889	0.300	1.760	1.162	2.323	3.611	5.722	3.241	0.000
10	81.202	0.300	1.760	1.162	1.162	3.595	5.464	3.209	0.000
11	88.515	0.300	1.760	1.162	1.162	3.579	5.464	3.209	0.000
12	95.828	0.300	1.760	1.162	1.162	3.563	5.334	3.193	0.000
13	103.141	0.300	1.760	1.162	1.162	3.547	5.205	3.177	0.000
14	110.454	0.300	1.760	1.162	1.162	3.531	5.075	3.161	0.000
15	117.767	0.300	1.760	1.162	1.162	3.515	4.946	3.145	0.000
16	125.080	0.300	1.760	1.162	1.162	3.499	4.817	3.129	0.000

ELEVATION OF THE PYLON'S
HORIZONTAL SECTIONS

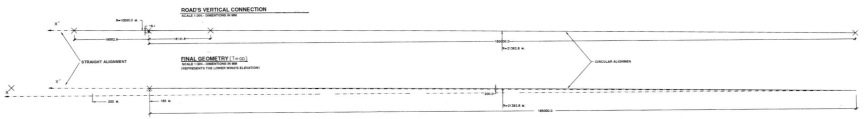

Fig. C.4

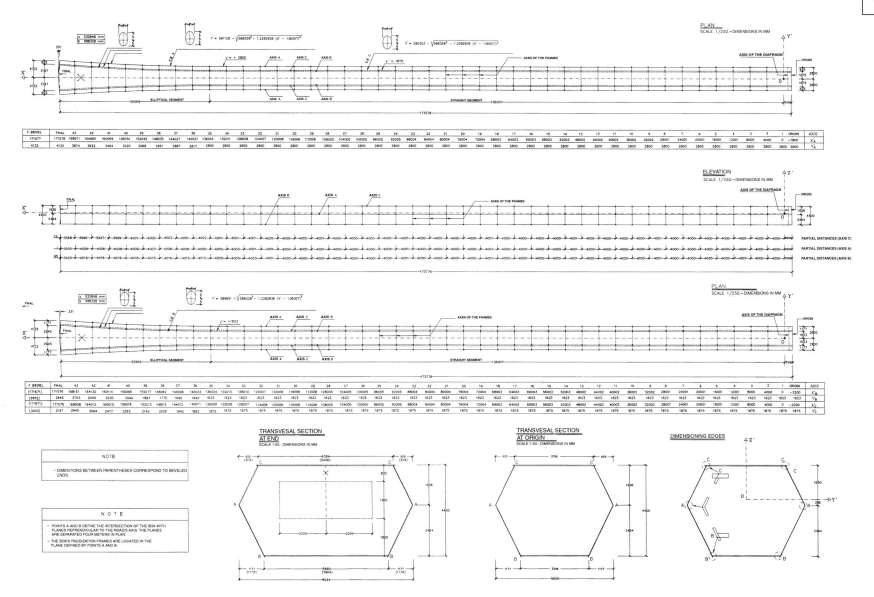

Fig. C.5

Fig. C.6

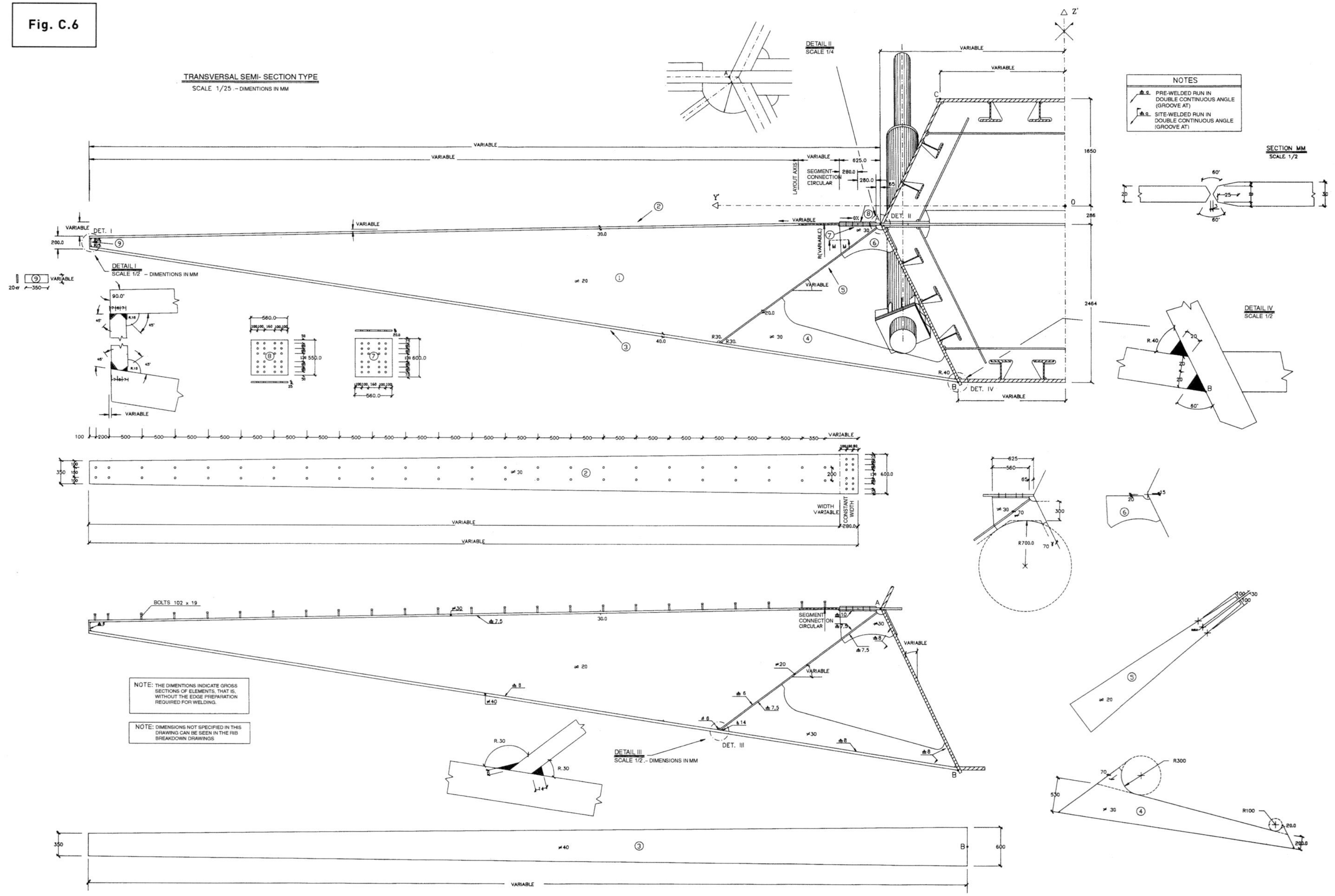
TRANSVERSAL SEMI- SECTION TYPE
SCALE 1/25 .- DIMENTIONS IN MM
NOTES
PRE-WELDED RUN IN DOUBLE CONTINUOUS ANGLE (GROOVE AT)
SITE-WELDED RUN IN DOUBLE CONTINUOUS ANGLE (GROOVE AT)
DETAIL II
SCALE 1/4
SECTION MM
SCALE 1/2
DETAIL I
SCALE 1/2 - DIMENTIONS IN MM
DETAIL IV
SCALE 1/2
LAYOUT AXIS
SEGMENT CONNECTION CIRCULAR
VARIABLE
WIDTH VARIABLE
CONSTANT WIDTH
BOLTS 102 x 19
NOTE: THE DIMENTIONS INDICATE GROSS SECTIONS OF ELEMENTS, THAT IS, WITHOUT THE EDGE PREPARATION REQUIRED FOR WELDING.
NOTE: DIMENSIONS NOT SPECIFIED IN THIS DRAWING CAN BE SEEN IN THE RIB BREAKDOWN DRAWINGS
DETAIL III
SCALE 1/2.- DIMENSIONS IN MM
DET. I
DET. II
DET. III
DET. IV

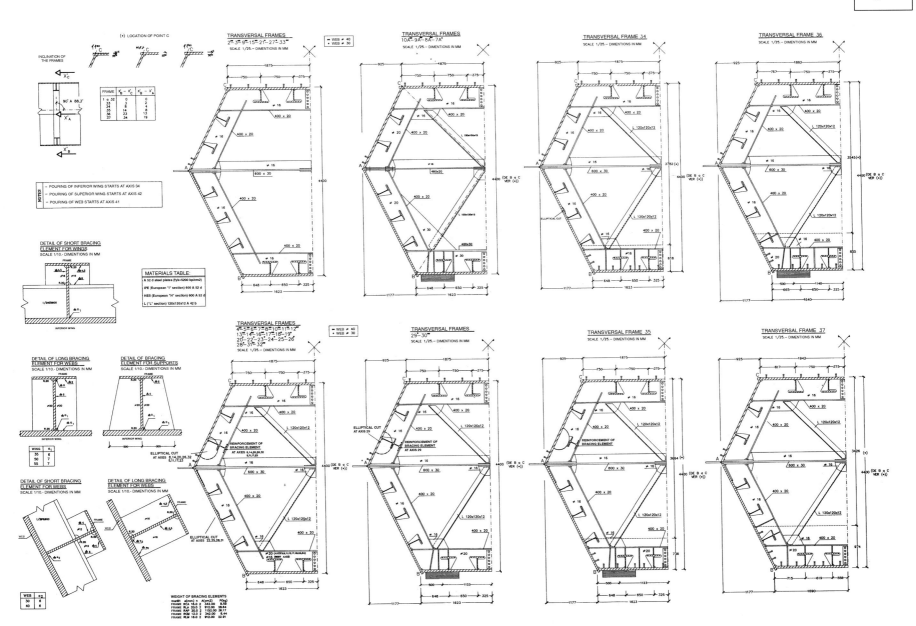

Fig. C.7

Fig. C.8

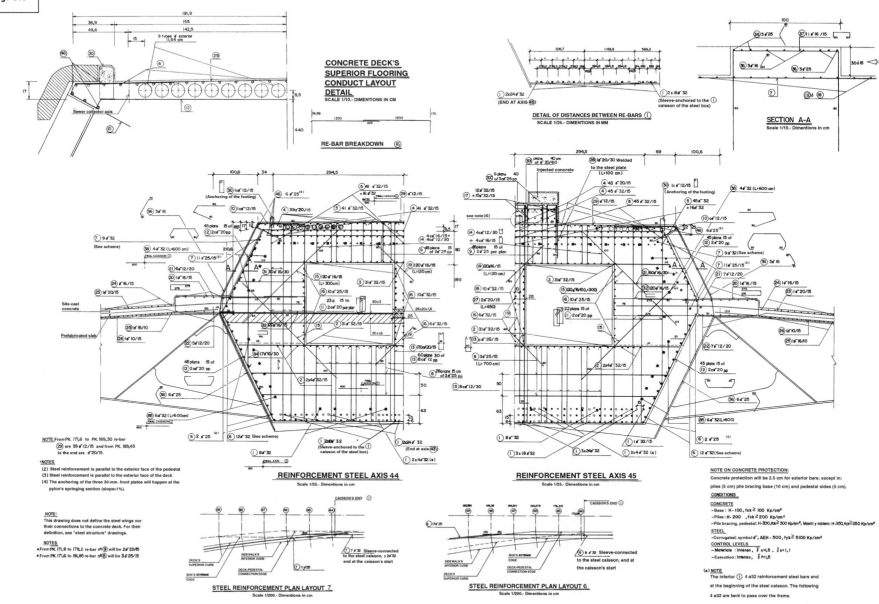

CONCRETE DECK'S SUPERIOR FLOORING CONDUCT LAYOUT DETAIL
SCALE 1/10.- DIMENTIONS IN CM

RE-BAR BREAKDOWN (16)

DETAIL OF DISTANCES BETWEEN RE-BARS (1)
SCALE 1/25.- DIMENTIONS IN MM

SECTION A-A
Scale 1/10.- Dimentions in cm

REINFORCEMENT STEEL AXIS 44
Scale 1/25.- Dimentions in cm

REINFORCEMENT STEEL AXIS 45
Scale 1/25.- Dimentions in cm

STEEL REINFORCEMENT PLAN LAYOUT 7
Scale 1/200.- Dimentions in cm

STEEL REINFORCEMENT PLAN LAYOUT 6
Scale 1/200.- Dimentions in cm

NOTE: From PK. 171,6 to PK. 189,30 re-bar (29) are 119 ∅12/15 and from PK. 189,45 to the end are ∅20/15.

·NOTES
(2) Steel reinforcement is parallel to the exterior face of the pedestal
(3) Steel reinforcement is parallel to the exterior face of the deck
(4) The anchoring of the three 30-mm. front plates will happen at the pylon's springing section (slope=1%).

NOTE:
This drawing does not define the steel wings nor their connections to the concrete deck. For their definition, see "steel structure" drawings.

NOTES
• From PK. 171,6 to 178,2 re-bar nº(9) will be 2∅ 25/15
• From PK. 171,6 to 191,85 re-bar nº(8) will be 3∅ 25/15

NOTE ON CONCRETE PROTECTION:
Concrete protection will be 2.5 cm for exterior bars; except in: piles (5 cm) pile bracing base (10 cm) and pedestal sides (5 cm).

CONDITIONS
CONCRETE
- Base : H- 100, fck $\geq$ 100 Kp/cm²
- Piles: H- 200 , fck $\geq$ 200 Kp/cm²
- Pile bracing, pedestal: H-300,fck $\geq$ 300 Kp/cm²; Mastil y tablero: H-350,fck $\geq$ 350 Kp/cm²
STEEL
- Corrugated: symbol ∅, AEH - 500, fyk $\geq$ 5100 Kp/cm²
CONTROL LEVELS
- Materials : Intense, γ c=1,5 , γ s=1,1
- Execution: Intense, γ f=1,5

(∗) NOTE
The inferior (1) 4 ∅32 reinforcement steel bars end at the beginning of the steel caisson. The following 4 ∅32 are bent to pass over the frame.

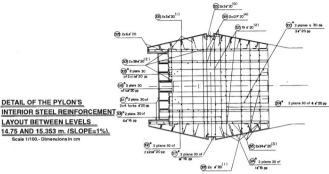

DETAIL OF THE PYLON'S INTERIOR STEEL REINFORCEMENT LAYOUT BETWEEN LEVELS 14.75 AND 15.353 m. (SLOPE=1%).
Scale 1/100.- Dimensions in cm

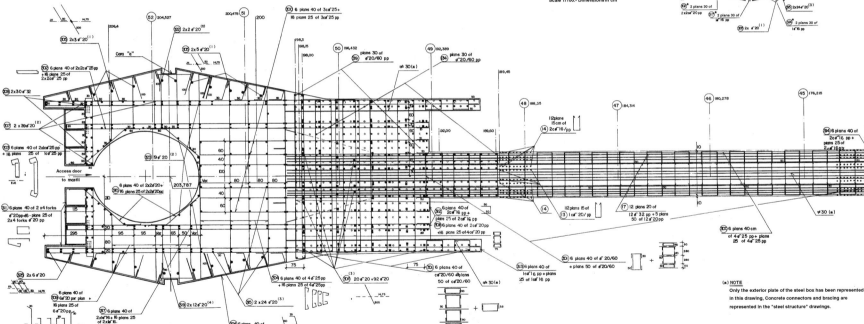

HORIZONTAL SECTION, Z=15,353 (P=1%), IV-IV (CAISSON I)
Scale 1/50.- Dimensions in cm

Fig. C.9

NOTES ON BAR OVERLAPPING:

Bar diameter (mm)	Connection length (cm)
⌀ 16	60
⌀ 20	100
⌀ 25	150

● All overlapping can be executed at 100%

● The overlapping of bars 300, 302, 303 and 304 will be excuted with the utmost care, meeting always the minimum overlapping distances indicated in the preceding table.

NOTES
(1) Re-bar 305 will be parallel to the pylon's side faces
(2) Re-bars 307, 323 and 325 will be parallel to the back face of the pylon in the longitudinal dimension and vertical in the transversal direction.
(3) Re-bar 315 and 306 will be parallel to the front face of the pylon in the longitudinal dimension and vertical in the transversal direction.
(4) Re-bar 318 will be inclined 58.377 degrees in the longitudinal dimension and vertical in the transversal direction.
(0) Re-bar parallel to face "a"

(a) NOTE
Only the exterior plate of the steel box has been represented in this drawing. Concrete connectors and bracing are represented in the "steel structure" drawings.

NOTE ON THE CONCRETE PROTECTION:
Concrete protection will be 2.5 cm for exterior bars

CONDITIONS
CONCRETE
- Pylon : H-350, fck ≥ 350 Kp/cm²

STEEL
- Corrugated: symbol ⌀ , AEH-500, fyk ≥ 5100 Kp/cm²
CONTROL LEVELS
- Materials : Intense, γ_c=1,5 , γ_s=1,1
- Execution : Intense, γ_f=1,5

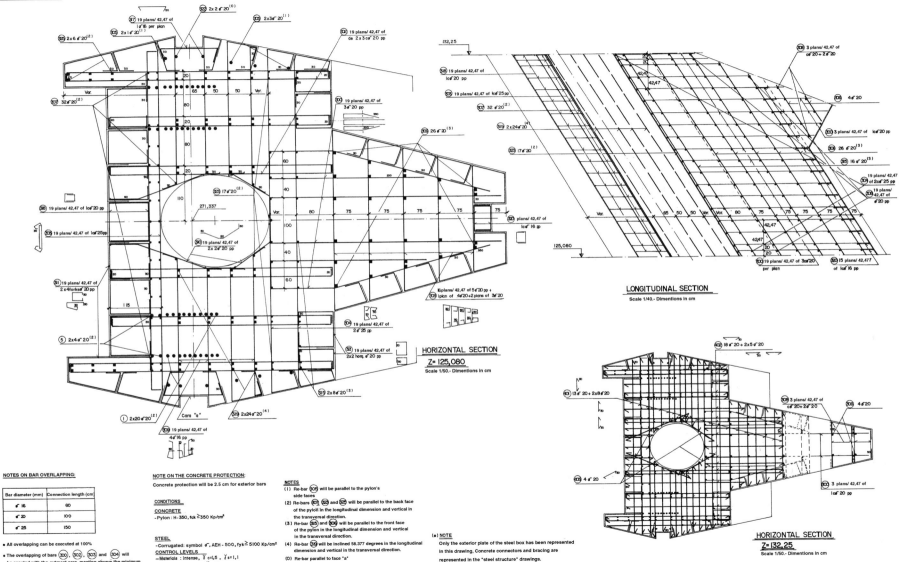

Fig. C.10

HORIZONTAL SECTION
Z= 125,080
Scale 1/50.- Dimentions in cm

LONGITUDINAL SECTION
Scale 1/40.- Dimentions in cm

HORIZONTAL SECTION
Z= 132,25
Scale 1/50.- Dimentions in cm

NOTES ON BAR OVERLAPPING:

Bar diameter (mm)	Connection length (cm)
∅ 16	60
∅ 20	100
∅ 25	150

• All overlapping can be executed at 100%

• The overlapping of bars 300, 302, 303 and 304 will
be excuted with the outmost care, meeting always the minimum
overlapping distances indicated in the preceding table.

NOTE ON THE CONCRETE PROTECTION:

Concrete protection will be 2.5 cm for exterior bars

CONDITIONS

CONCRETE
- Pylon : H-350, fck ≥ 350 Kp/cm²

STEEL
- Corrugated : symbol ∅, AEH - 500, fyk ≥ 5100 Kp/cm²
CONTROL LEVELS
- Materials : intense , γc=1,5 , γs=1,1
- Execution : intense, γf=1,5

NOTES
(1) Re-bar 305 will be parallel to the pylon's
side faces
(2) Re-bars 307, 323 and 325 will be parallel to the back face
of the pylon in the longitudinal dimension and vertical in
the transversal direction.
(3) Re-bars 315 and 308 will be parallel to the front face
of the pylon in the longitudinal dimension and vertical
in the transversal direction.
(4) Re-bar 319 will be inclined 58.377 degrees in the longitudinal
dimension and vertical in the transversal direction.
(0) Re-bar parallel to face "a"

(a) NOTE
Only the exterior plate of the steel box has been represented
in this drawing, Concrete connectors and bracing are
represented in the "steel structure" drawings.

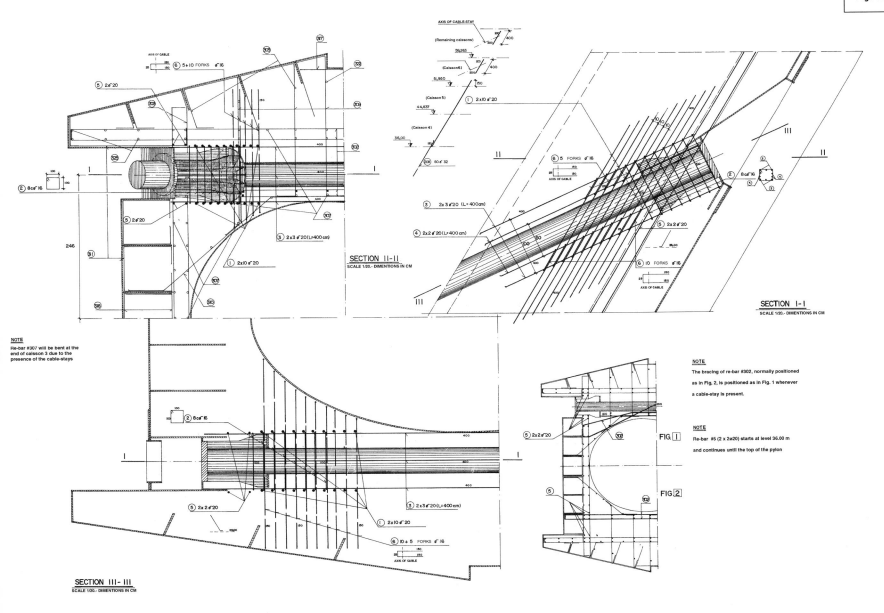

Fig. C.11

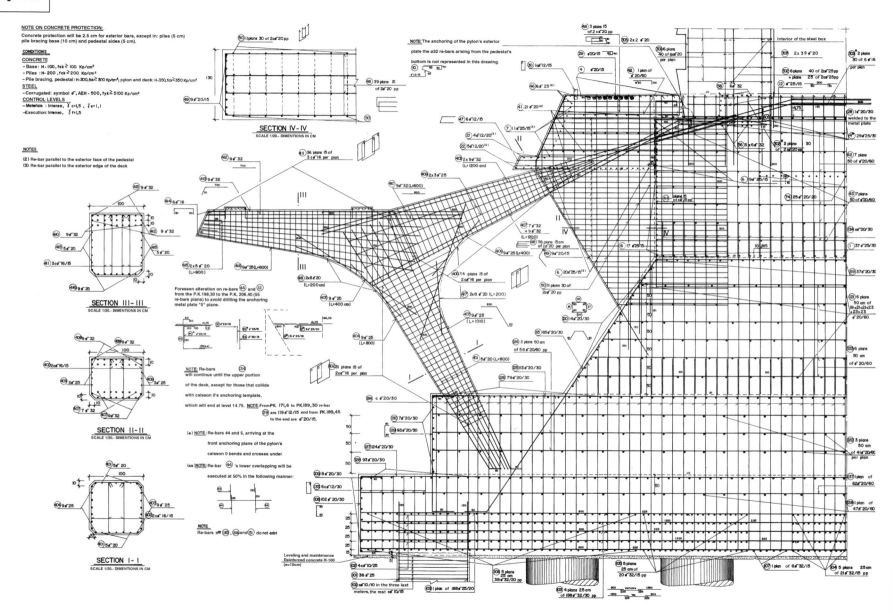

Fig. C.12

Fig. C.13

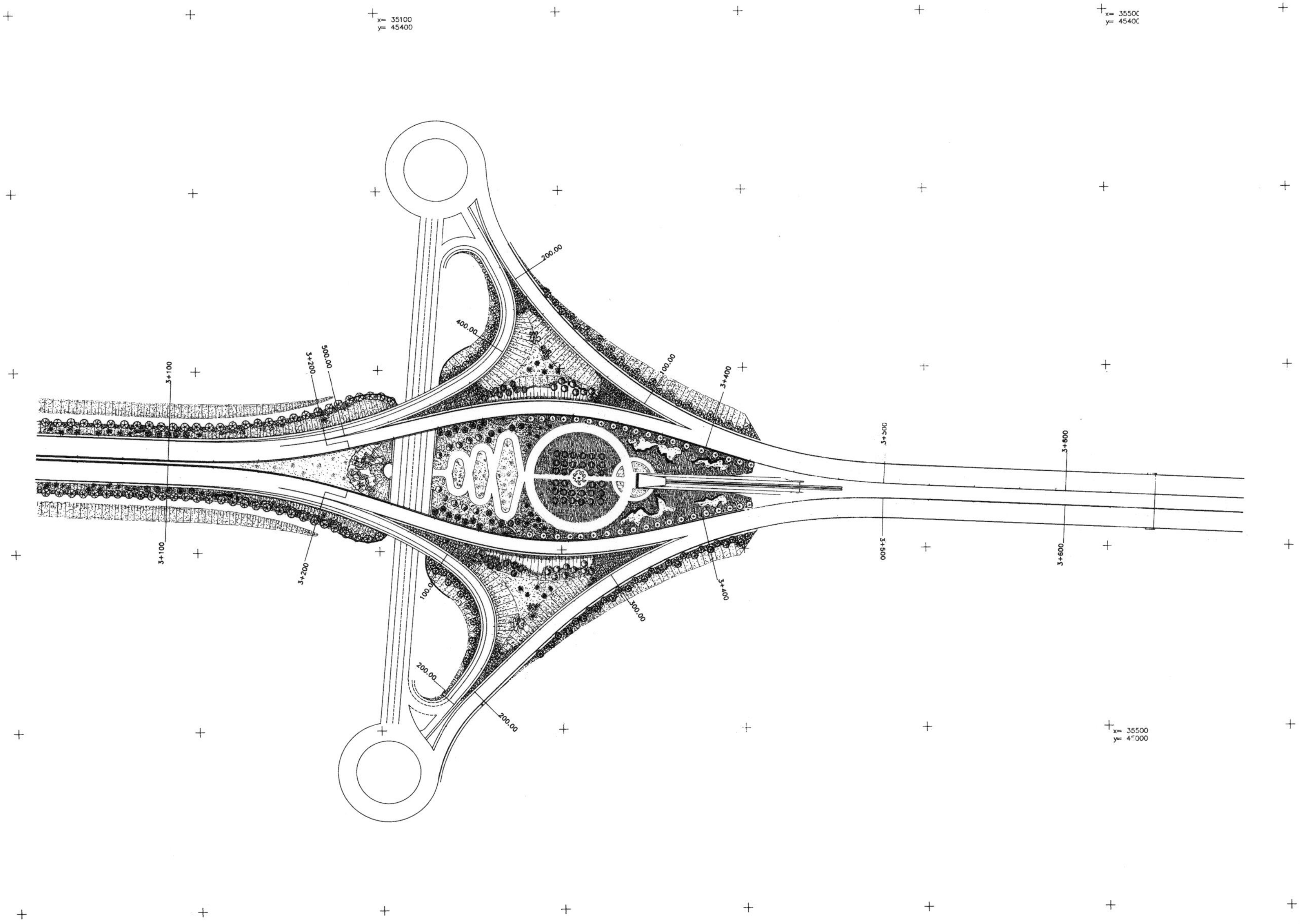

REFERENCES

Alonso-Cobo, Carlos, and José Ramón Atienza-Reales. N. d. (a). "Paso del Alamillo Camas-San Lázaro II, Proyecto de Construcción, Junta de Andalucía."

Alonso-Cobo, Carlos, and José Ramón Atienza-Reales. N. d. (b). "Paso del Alamillo Camas-San Lázaro II, Anejo de Cálculos, Junta de Andalucía."

Alonso-Cobo, Carlos, José R. Atienza-Reales, and Angel C. Aparicio. 1993. "Construction of the Alamillo Bridge in Seville." FIP Notes. *Quarterly Journal of the Fédération Internationale de la Précontraire* (February), pp. 16–21.

Asencio, Javier, and Luis Peset. 1992. "El Puente del Alamillo." SYGMA 8, Dragados, Dirección Técnica, June 1992, pp. 20–39.

Davenport, A. G. 1970. "On the Statistical Prediction of Structural Performance in a Wind Environment." In *Proceedings of a Seminar on Wind Loads on Structures,* Honolulu, October 19–24, 1970, pp. 325–342.

Diaz-Hermidas, Alberto. 1994. "Managing Change and Conflict in Architectural Projects: Four Pavilions in Seville's Expo '92." Doctoral dissertation, Harvard University, Graduate School of Design, Cambridge, MA.

Fomento de Construcciones y Contratas, S. A. 1992a. "Viaducto de la Cartuja, Sevilla." Informe Técnico 204, Servicio Técnico, Departamento de Métodos, January 1992.

Fomento de Construcciones y Contratas, S. A. 1992b. "Puente del Alamillo, Sevilla." Informe Técnico 205, Servicio Técnico, Departamento de Métodos, January 1992.

King, J. P. C. , G. L. Larose, and A. G. Davenport. 1991. *A Study of Wind Effects for the Paso del Alamillo Bridge, Sevilla, Spain.* BLWT-SS28–1991, August 1991.

Menn, Christian. 1991. *Architecture: Design Implementation,* ed. S. N. Pollalis. American Collegiate Schools of Architecture, 10th Technology Conference, Cambridge, Massachusetts.

Nolli, Aldo. 1987. "Trail Sign—Santiago Calatrava: Bridge in Barcelona." *Lotus International,* no. 564, pp. 62–73.

Pollalis, S. N., and Y. J. Bakos. 1996. "Technology in the Design Process." *Journal of Architectural and Planning Research* 13, no. 2 (Summer).

Terzaghi, K. 1955. "Evaluation of Coefficient of Subgrade Reaction." *Geotechnique* 5, no. 4 (December), pp. 297–326.